LINDSAY BRADSHAW'S

ONE HOUR

Party
Cakes

Aleta Show
12 Builnecrag St.

LINDSAY BRADSHAW'S
ONE HOUR
Party Cakes

MEREHURST

Edited by Gillian Haslam
Designed by Christine Wood
Photography by Clive Streeter

Published 1994 by Merehurst Limited
Ferry House
51–57 Lacy Road
Putney
London SW15 1PR

A catalogue record for this book is available from the
British Library
ISBN 1 85391 044 9 (hardback)
ISBN 1 85391 461 4 (paperback)

Typeset by J&L Composition Ltd, UK
Colour separation by Fotographics Ltd, UK–Hong Kong
Printed by Leefung–Asco Printers Ltd, China

ACKNOWLEDGEMENTS

Cake Art Ltd, Venture Way, Crown Estate,
Priorswood, Taunton, Somerset TA2 8DE

Filtering Media Manufacturers, Unit 5, Kings Park,
Primrose Hill, Kings Langley, Herts WD4 8ST

G. T. Culpitt & Son Ltd, Culpitt House, Place Farm,
Wheathampstead, Herts AL4 8SB

Guy Paul & Co Ltd, Unit B4, Foundry Way, Little
End Road, Eaton Socon, Cambs PE19 3JH

J. F. Renshaw Ltd, Mitcham House, River Court,
Albert Drive, Woking, Surrey GU21 5RP

Squires Kitchen, Squires House, 3 Waverley Lane,
Farnham, Surrey GU9 8BB

The Icing Shop, 259A Orrell Road, Orrell, Wigan
WN5 8NB

CONTENTS

INTRODUCTION

To have been drawn to the title of this book and now be reading the introduction no doubt means that you enjoy decorating cakes, and the idea of quick-to-decorate ones, for one reason or another, appeals to you. As a demonstrator I am often asked to show quick methods and short cuts for making cake decoration less time-consuming, particularly for non-professional groups who want to enjoy cake decorating, make it fun and produce an edible creation that people will admire and ultimately find delicious to eat. Having been shown a selection of quick-to-make-cakes, audiences are quite amazed at what can be achieved with ready-made this and plastic that on a bought cake, and are even more astonished at the small amount of time involved, making the ideas realistically possible for people leading busy lives.

This book is ideal for anyone who tends always to buy a party cake purely because they don't have the time (or that's what they think) to make one. Obviously, practised hands will be able to work more quickly than those less experienced, but by taking a few short cuts, such as using good quality ready-made cake bases, covering pastes and cake decorations, anyone can make and decorate a cake. All the cakes shown in this book are covered and decorated using sugarpaste, renowned for its ease of use and creative possibilities and each cake has been designed to use the minimum of specialist equipment. So now you've no excuse not to make a cake, even at a minute's notice. Don't feel that you are cheating by using shop-bought items.

Provided you shop around and purchase good quality materials, this book will show you, step-by-step, how to make an edible masterpiece to be proud of, giving you a real sense of satisfaction and achievement.

I also hope that cake decorators, both professional and amateur, especially those running a celebration cake business either as part of a bakery and confectionery or as a home-based enterprise, will find the ideas in this book a source of inspiration for quick-to-make, cost-effective cakes that could command a good price. And for the keen sugar-crafter, even though the cakes are intended as quick-to-do, you can still be a perfectionist. The selection of cakes has been designed to cater for all occasions using a wide variety of colours, textures, techniques and imaginative shapes. Each can be finished in one hour and many can be completed in less than half that time, but there's nothing to stop you taking longer and enhancing them even more, adding extra details or replacing commercial decorations with hand-made items. Make life easier for yourself by taking a few minutes to read the recipe and method, plan your time and prepare your ingredients and equipment before starting work – make cake decorating a fun experience and enjoy yourself!

Happy quick cake decorating.

Lindsay

EQUIPMENT

For some people, the commercial 'bandwagon' has spoiled their cake decorating, especially when they are told by a teacher or sales assistant that they really need specialist tools and equipment, and that a particular technique cannot be carried out without it. I go along with this in many cases, and having the right tools for the job in hand does make life easier. However, with a little thought and selectiveness, you can save yourself considerable expense and a kitchen drawer full of redundant items that you may only use once.

I have purposely designed the majority of cakes in the book to require the minimum of special equipment and most only require basic kitchen items that you probably already have, such as a rolling pin, small knife, palette knife, cutting board and pastry brush. When special items of equipment are specified in the list, please don't immediately dash out and buy them. More often than not you can use or at least adapt another item from the kitchen cupboard or technique to achieve a similar effect. Here are just a few such adaptations that may inspire you and will certainly save you money.

TOOL	ALTERNATIVE
Garrett frill cutter	Use a large scone cutter or fluted round cutter.
Rib rolling pin	Roll out sugarpaste and indent equally spaced parallel lines using a plastic ruler.
Broderie cutter	Create the desired pattern combination of holes using a No. 2, 3 or 4 plain writing tube (tip).
Clay gun	Roll out the sugarpaste thinly or in ropes, then twist and/or cut to create the desired shape.
Cutters	Simply draw or trace the required shape onto thin card and cut out to use as a template to cut around.
Sphere tin	Bake the cake in a pudding basin and when cool, sculpt to a rounder shape using a sharp knife dipped in warm water.
Ball modelling tool	Make a similar tool by sanding the blunt end of a wooden meat skewer to make a rounded shape.

You will probably already have most of the tools and equipment required to make the cakes in this book in your kitchen drawer. A few of the cakes require special items, as shown here.

BASIC EQUIPMENT

For the majority of finishes shown on the cakes in this book you will need the following basic equipment to get started:

Cutting board

Rolling pin

Small knife for cutting shapes and trimming

Medium-sized palette knife

Small brush

Icing sugar for dusting when rolling

Although a turntable does make it easier to manoeuvre the cake whilst decorating it, it is not essential for the cakes featured.

If you do get hooked by cake decorating, which is likely as it is quite addictive, be very selective when you shop and only buy those items that are essential to your work. As you progress, your experienced eye will soon establish that many cutters and tools have more than one use.

CAKE BOARDS

As a way of incorporating more colour and interest to your finished cake, with the minimum of work, you should try some of the board-covering ideas featured in this book. Covering the cake board with decorative paper still creates an attractive, finished look to your creation but eliminates the need to cover the board with sugarpaste and probably crimp the edges, and you will have realised already that the former method is less expensive.

Though the recipes suggest a particular board finish, you can quite easily change it to suit your own preferences and the time you have available. To cover a board with paper, simply cut the chosen paper about 3cm (1¼in) larger than the actual board. If using decorative gift wrapping paper, you will need to glue it to the board using a non-toxic glue (the stick-type ones are usually the best for this job). Self-adhesive laminate, the type used for shelves and covering books, is not as messy as glue can be and is certainly easier to work with. Turn the paper neatly over the board edge and secure on the reverse side of the board. For round and other curved shapes, pull and pleat the paper as you go around the board to create a neat finish.

Shop around in stationers, card and gift shops to find the nicest papers – you will enjoy matching and co-ordinating the coverings to the cake and you can create exactly the look you wish from stripy, spotty, flowery or sophisticated papers.

If time and your budget allows, give your covered cake boards an extra special touch by edging with gold or silver banding or satin or velvet ribbon. Each can be quickly and cleanly attached using a non-toxic stick-type adhesive or a narrow length of double-sided adhesive tape.

> ### T I P
> If in any doubt about the colours migrating from the board-covering paper to the cake, place a piece of waxed paper cut to the size and shape of the cake between the two.

Cake boards can be used as they are or, for a more attractive finish, cover them with decorative foils or gift wrapping paper and trim the edge with banding or ribbon.

COMMERCIALLY AVAILABLE INGREDIENTS AND DECORATIONS

To get the greatest benefit from the quick-to-decorate concept, you really should cut out the fuss and buy in as much ready-made material and decoration as you can without sacrificing every bit of hand-crafted work and making the cake look cheap or mass-produced. Use what time you have available to actually cover, quickly dress and trim the cake, almost instantly, rather than spending hours mixing your own sugarpaste, making flowers and doing lots of laborious decoration. For fun and novelty cakes certainly, you'll probably find the last-minute or impulse cakes are more stunning than those planned in advance, and more importantly you'll also have more fun doing them!

SUGARPASTE

With the standard of consistent product, improved flavour and wide range of ready-coloured pastes now available in sugarcraft shops and supermarkets, it really isn't worth weighing ingredients, warming and mixing your own. You can buy sugarpaste in

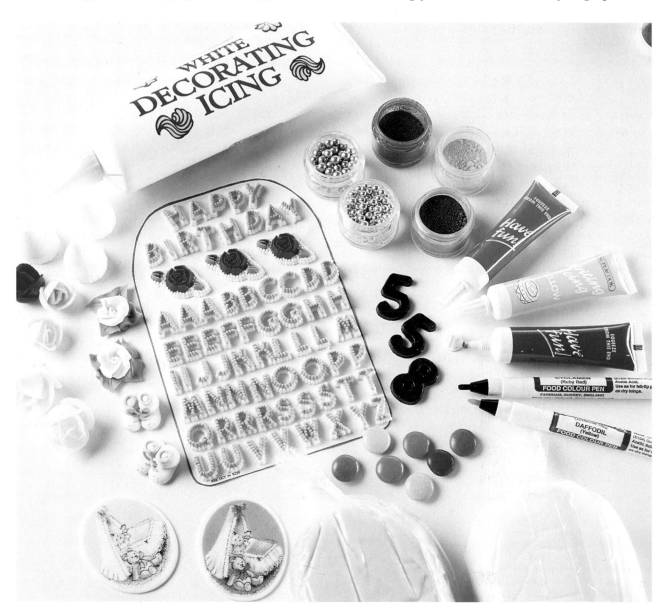

white and a host of useful pale tints and also in strong colours – even black – so there's something suitable for all occasions. The sugarpaste is conveniently packed in small retail packs. If, however, you use a lot, you may be able to negotiate a good discount for bulk buying.

PASTILLAGE

Just a few of the recipes in the book need pastillage – a hard-setting paste used for modelling. Again, it really isn't worth making your own. Buy an instant dry mix type that you simply mix with water. Alternatively, for its uses in this book, you could knead 1 tsp gum tragacanth powder into 500g (1lb) sugarpaste.

DECORATIONS

The increased interest in cake decoration over the past few years has really kept manufacturers on their toes, and there is now a better range of cake decorations more widely available than ever before. At first glance, the majority of plastic and fabric decorations may look cheap and very artificial, but with a little thought given to their application and indeed probably some modification or adaptation, you can make great use of anything from plastic lettering, numerals and bells to fabric butterflies, flowers and leaves. The secret is not to use the items as they are straight from the pack – tweak the flowers, curve the leaves, trim the lettering to suit and then attach them to your cake and you'll be surprised at the difference! Fabric, wafer and piped icing flowers, all available commercially, will benefit from a quick tint with dusting powder, just to make them more individual. Writing on cakes is usually the most difficult part so take advantage of the many cut out letters, numbers and popular inscriptions that are available, and don't forget ribbons, bows and cake candles – birthday cakes aren't the same without colourful ribbon trimmings and candles to blow out. If you think sticking candles in your cake will spoil the look of it, insert them just before the party.

Edible decorations are becoming increasingly popular and you can now obtain everything from lettering and hand-made flowers to printed plaques and ready-made icing in tubes.

There is a wide range of bought plastic lettering available.

The design and quality of plastic decorations has improved considerably. There is now also a greater range of fabric flowers, leaves, beads and ribbons to choose from.

> ### TIP
> Don't attempt to decorate a cake that is beyond your level of skill. It is far better to give a neat finish to a simple cake with bought decorations, rather than struggle to perfect a more intricate hand-made design.

MAKING AND BAKING

If you are in a hurry and haven't got time to bake, skip this section and go to page 13. If, however, you do have the time, there's nothing nicer than a home-made cake. Nowadays, with the vast array of cookery books and the many magazines that feature good, easy-to-follow recipes, it is simple to select all the cake-baking ingredients you require from your sugarcraft shop or supermarket. There is, of course, the washing up, but the flavour and texture of your freshly baked cake will prove well worth the time and effort.

If you do bake your own cake but haven't much time, valuable minutes, and sometimes hours, can still be saved in several ways, for instance by using the popular all-in type method for sponge cake or by greasing and flouring cake tins (pans) rather than lining with greaseproof paper which can be quite fiddly, especially with some of the more

intricate shaped tins. For fruit cakes, buy ready-washed and selected dried fruit, currants, sultanas, raisins and so on from a supplier with a fairly rapid turnover so that you know the product is fresh and in most instances the fruit is sufficiently moist to use without pre-soaking.

If these tips still don't tempt you to start baking, help is at hand as you can now purchase good quality dry cake mixes (you do need to shop around and be choosy) to which you just add water or egg, mix and bake. The best ready mixes are those used by the professional baker and confectioner and, until recently, these weren't available to the general

Save yourself time and work by using commercially available cake bases for your celebration cake. There is a wide variety of types and sizes that you can choose from.

TIP
To speed up the cooling of your freshly baked cake, allow it to cool a little then place it on a wire cooling rack in your refrigerator until cool enough to decorate.

public. However, with the upsurge of the numerous home-based celebration cake businesses, many bakers and confectioners have found the cake decorating side of their own business slowing down. As a result they have diversified to maintain turnover by selling retail packs of these top quality mixes. You'll probably find that your local sugarcraft shop also sells a range of plain, chocolate and fruit cake mixes. Supermarkets sell a wide range of mixes, but they cater only for small cakes and sandwich cakes so you'll probably need two, three or more packets to make a decent-sized sponge for a celebration.

A few of the ideas in this book feature cakes baked in special shaped tins, such as spheres and domes. You can buy these at good sugarcraft shops or for a 'one-off' cake, most similar shops offer a hire service, where you can borrow the tin for a day or two. The tins are easy to use and just need greasing and flouring to prevent the cake sticking. A guide as to the amount of mixture required for these tins will be found on the packaging or the sales assistant should be sufficiently knowledgeable to offer advice.

If you are taking up cake decorating as a hobby or starting a small business, or even if you are just making the odd celebration cake, as people see your cake creations you'll no doubt be asked regularly to make them for friends and relatives, so it is a good idea to batch-bake occasionally. When stocking up your freezer in this way with the more popular shapes and sizes of sponge cake, label and date them so they are ready for defrosting for those last-minute requests. If you are baking the cake for use without freezing, try to plan your cake baking day 24 hours before you intend to decorate. Allowing the baked cake to stand produces a firmer, easier to handle cake. Simply wrap the cooled cake in polythene until ready for use.

Fruit cakes can also be made well in advance, in fact they improve with keeping providing they are stored correctly. You should not freeze fruit cake. Simply wrap it in greaseproof paper and then place in loose polythene to allow the cake to breathe a little. Brush the cake from time to time with rum or brandy to keep the cake moist and to improve the flavour and texture.

COMMERCIALLY AVAILABLE CAKE BASES

More often than not, decorating cakes is the part of cake making that most appeals to people, and while many like baking, the thought of weighing ingredients, mixing them, lining tins, baking and the waiting time while the cake cools – not to mention the washing up – actually discourages some would-be cake decorators from having a go. As with most problems, help is at hand as your local baker and confectioner, good supermarkets and, for businesses, cash and carry outlets, usually offer a wide range of plain, chocolate, lightly fruited and rich fruit cake bases, all undecorated and in various shapes and sizes. Providing you seek out the best quality ones, you're halfway towards making your edible work of art. If you intend to decorate cakes fairly regularly, and you know that availability at your supplier is not consistent, it is wise to buy in a stock of the cake bases you will use most. These can be wrapped in a suitable covering or labelled in a container and stored in the freezer until required. As you receive a request or order for a particular cake, simply remove from the freezer and defrost on a wire rack ready for decorating. Fruit cakes can remain in the packaging in which they were purchased, which usually will carry brief storage instructions for you to follow.

TIP

Look for sponge cakes that are firm but moist and that will not crumble when you start cutting and shaping – this is especially important when creating intricate shapes.
Fruit cakes need to be of a good shape and moist with a mellow flavour. Once you find a good brand or supplier, keep to it.

PREPARING THE CAKE

Preparing the cake is a most important part of cake decorating work. Careful handling, cutting and neat layering all contribute to making an accurate cake base on which to build and they also provide a visually pleasing appearance to the cake when cut.

SPONGE CAKES

Ideally freshly baked cakes should be stored (not refrigerated) for approximately 12 hours before beginning work with them. It is particularly important to store them before cutting. When the cake has cooled, wrap it loosely in a polythene sheet. This storage period allows the crumb to close a little and the cake as a whole to firm up, thus enabling easier handling. Ready-made shop-bought cake bases do not require a firming period and can be used straight away. Frozen cakes can be used immediately they have defrosted, although if you have any intricate cutting to do, do this before the cake has fully defrosted as the firmness will make it easier to produce a neater shape. Before cutting, layering or masking of any kind, remove the thin crust or 'skin' of the cake by drawing the back edge of a long knife across the cake. Alternatively, use a sharp serrated knife in a conventional manner. Having prepared the cake, you can then spread the top and sides with buttercream or jam before covering with sugarpaste.

FRUIT CAKES

Prepare these in the conventional manner by first moistening and flavouring with a brushing of brandy or rum. Cover the cake's top and sides with a layer of almond marzipan, attaching it to the cake with boiled apricot jam to act as an adhesive. To cover the cake with sugarpaste, follow the method on page 15 but instead of attaching the sugarpaste with buttercream or jam, simply brush the marzipan covering with a little gin or vodka.

Prepare fruit cakes in the conventional manner, covering top and sides with a layer of almond marzipan. To stick the sugarpaste on, brush the marzipan lightly with alcohol.

QUICK-TO-DO CAKE COVERING

The sugarpaste referred to in each recipe for covering the cakes and boards is commercially available in a ready-to-roll form. The paste can be bought either in white, which allows you to produce your own colours, or ready-coloured in a limited but popular range of tints.

COLOURING SUGARPASTE

To colour the paste, simply add the desired colouring. Paste colours give the best results and you can obtain strong colours without softening the paste, as would be the result if liquid colours were used. Add the colouring to the sugarpaste using a cocktail stick (toothpick) and knead thoroughly until evenly distributed. While you are working and in particular during storage, keep any unused paste covered with polythene to prevent it drying out.

CAKES

Having coloured the paste, it is ready to roll out. If you are using white paste, it will require a short kneading time to soften it and make it more pliable. Prepare the cake by covering with a thin spreading of buttercream or jam to act as an adhesive for the sugarpaste. Roll out sugarpaste on a flat, clean surface such as a kitchen worktop or a large cutting

board dusted with icing (confectioner's) sugar. Pick up the paste by sliding your hands, palms uppermost, underneath it and lifting it onto the cake. Carefully remove your hands, allowing the paste to drape loosely over the cake. Slightly curve one hand and tease the paste smoothly over the cake, removing any creases and folds as you go. Trim off any excess paste from the base using a small knife, then use a smoother or flat plastic scraper to make a clean, neat, flawless surface. Set the cake aside or transfer onto a cake board ready for decoration. The technique is basically the same for all shapes of cakes, although with some of the more intricate shapes, such as petal and hexagon, it may take more time to achieve a good finish.

Pick up the sugarpaste by sliding your hands underneath and lift onto the cake. Drape the paste loosely on the cake and smooth from the centre to remove any air pockets.

Having cut and layered the cake with cream and/or jam and removed any unwanted crust, spread the cake top and sides with a thin layer of apricot jam, ready for covering in sugarpaste.

After removing creases and folds, use a small knife to trim excess paste from the base.

TIP

To create an attractive sheen on the sugarpaste, remove any remaining particles of excess icing sugar by 'polishing' the surface with the palm of your hand in a gentle rotating motion. The same method can be used on sugarpasted cake boards.

If you prefer the flavour or handling qualities of buttercream instead of jam, it will still do the same job of acting as an adhesive to stick the sugarpaste to the cake.

Use a smoother or flat plastic scraper to create a clean, neat, flawless surface. Smoothing needs to be done immediately after covering and before the paste skins.

Prepare the cake board by brushing with water to make the sugarpaste stick. Don't wet the board, simply moisten it, otherwise the paste will slide and slip rather than stick.

Cover the board using a similar technique as described for covering the cake. Smooth the surface to remove any air pockets and neatly trim the edges with a small knife.

The covered board can be left as it is, but for a more decorative finish use a crimping tool whilst the paste is still soft to create a fancy border around the edge.

TIP

Using the board covering method described, removing the cake-shaped portion will prevent the base of the cake coming into direct contact with the sugarpaste, which can cause the sugarpaste to discolour or sweat.

CAKE BOARDS

Covering cake boards with sugarpaste uses the same method as described for cakes (see page 15), except the cake board is lightly moistened with water to make the sugarpaste adhere. Trim off excess sugarpaste using a small knife. The board can be covered fully or you may prefer to make a template of the cake shape and cut away this area of sugarpaste before placing the cake on the board, securing it with dabs of royal icing. If the board edge is to be decorated with a crimping tool, this should be done while the sugarpaste is still soft. To give a more finished look to your cakes, attach a suitably coloured ribbon or silver or gold paper banding to the board edge at the last stage of decoration.

COLOURINGS

A wider variety of edible food colourings than ever before is now available, in liquid and paste form, powder and pens.

LIQUID COLOUR

Liquid colour has previously been restricted to being suitable mainly for producing pastel tints. If using such a weak colour solution, avoid trying to produce very dark shades as the amount of liquid required usually renders the royal icing (or sugarpaste) too soft to work with.

PASTE COLOUR

Available in a comprehensive range of colours, these are regarded as the best to use for colouring sugarpaste and royal icing. Use the tip of a cocktail stick (toothpick) to add the colour in small amounts until the desired tint or shade is produced.

DUSTING POWDER

This type, as the name implies, is mainly used in novelty cake work for dusting colour onto sugarpaste to create interesting effects. It is also used to tint leaves and the centres or petal edges of flowers. It can be used to colour royal icing, but as the intensity is not very strong it is uneconomical to use in large quantities.

ROYAL ICING

Used mainly for piping lettering and linework and for attaching decorations to cakes.

15g (½oz) albumen powder or albumen-based powder
90ml (3fl oz/⅓ cup) water
500g (1lb/4 cups) icing (confectioner's) sugar, finely sieved

Prepare the albumen powder with water according to the manufacturer's instructions. Strain the solution into a bowl. Add half the sugar, mixing well with a wooden spatula or spoon. Add the remaining sugar and continue mixing until all the icing sugar is incorporated. Scrape down the sides of the bowl, then lightly beat the mixture by hand or electric mixer until a definite bold peak is left when a spoonful of mixture is lifted from the bowl with a spatula. Store the icing in an airtight container until required. When in use, cover the bowl with a clean, moist cloth to prevent the icing crusting.

BUTTERCREAM

Used to sandwich cakes together, with or without a layer of jam. Buttercream, instead of jam, can also be spread thinly onto cakes as an adhesive medium for the sugarpaste covering.

185g (6oz/¾ cup) butter, softened
2 tbsp milk
375g (12oz/3 cups) icing (confectioner's) sugar
few drops of vanilla essence, to taste

Place the softened butter in a large bowl. Gradually add the milk, working the mixture together until creamy. For a less rich filling, a combination of soft butter and a quality margarine may be used, in which case less liquid will be required.

Sift the icing (confectioner's) sugar and gradually stir into the butter and milk mixture, then beat hard with a wooden spoon or electric mixer until pale, light and fluffy. A little extra liquid may be needed if a soft icing is required. Flavour as desired, with vanilla essence.

TRUFFLE PASTE

A firm paste ideal for moulding and shaping, this is particularly useful for difficult-to-shape pieces. The paste can be used as alternative to conventional sponge cake.

500g (1lb/8 cups) cake crumbs (see Note)
60g (2oz/⅓ cup) apricot jam
60ml (2fl oz/¼ cup) evaporated milk
½ tsp vanilla essence
about 125g (4oz) melted chocolate (see Note)

Place cake crumbs in bowl, add jam, evaporated milk and vanilla essence. Mix using a spoon then stream in melted chocolate and continue mixing until a firm paste is formed – a dry mix will crumble and be difficult to mould, while a mixture that is too soft will not retain its shape.

The prepared mixture will keep for a few days sealed in an airtight container in a refrigerator. To create shapes, simply mould using your hands dusted with icing (confectioner's) sugar. Attach shaped pieces to the main cake using jam, melted chocolate or buttercream.

Note If using chocolate cake crumbs, use milk or plain chocolate. For plain cake crumbs, use white chocolate. The amount of chocolate required varies depending whether the crumbs are dry or moist.

Truffle paste makes use of leftover cake trimmings which can be frozen in polythene bags. Freeze whole if to be used for forming shapes or crumb and sieve them for making truffle paste.

PREPARING TO DECORATE

In the following recipes, if a sponge cake has been used, the quantity of buttercream or jam for filling and masking (covering) the cake is your choice. For the filling, it is personal taste whether you like one layer of jam or buttercream or you may like to split the cake twice and fill with a layer of each to add colour and flavour. Jam and buttercream also do the same job of sticking the sugarpaste to the cake.

For the majority of recipes you will need a small amount of either water or reconstituted egg white powder or similar substitute for attaching various off-pieces and decorations to the main cake. For application use an appropriately sized brush.

RAG DOLLY

This attractive birthday cake will be popular with little girls as they will love the hair and ribbon bows.

23 × 18cm (9 × 7in) oval sponge cake
buttercream or jam for filling and masking
345g (11oz) lemon sugarpaste
440g (14oz) peachy-pink sugarpaste
220g (7oz) brown sugarpaste
15g (½oz) each of deep peach, white, black and red sugarpaste

EQUIPMENT
33 × 28cm (13 × 11in) oval cake board
crimping tool
paintbrush
2 ribbon bows

Use a template to cut out the two pieces of sugarpaste for the hair, marking the texture with the rounded tip of a paintbrush handle.

1 Split and sandwich the sponge cake with chosen filling and mask with buttercream or jam.

2 Roll out the lemon sugarpaste and use to cover the cake board, then crimp the edge while the paste is still soft (see page 70).

3 Roll out the peachy-pink sugarpaste and cover the cake. Place on the prepared board.

4 Roll out the brown sugarpaste and use the template on page 95 to cut out two hair shapes. Texture with the tip of a paintbrush handle. Make two plaits from the remaining paste as shown. Attach all parts to the cake.

5 Prepare the eyes, nose, mouth and cheeks as shown on page 95 and attach to the face. Pipe in some eyelashes if liked. Attach a ribbon bow to each plait with a dab of icing.

Cut out the eyes and cheeks from coloured sugarpaste and a long thin rope of red paste for the mouth. Model a small oval ball for the nose.

SPOTTY SNAKE

A colourful fun cake with a delicious cake mixture inside that children will love.

90g (3oz) tan coloured royal icing
75g (2½oz/½ cup) light brown sugar
1kg (2lb) truffle paste (see page 17)
500g (1lb) pink sugarpaste
60g (2oz) lemon sugarpaste
30g (1oz) green sugarpaste
7g (¼oz) each white, black and red sugarpaste

EQUIPMENT
28cm (11in) round cake board
2 small graduated round cutters
90cm (1yd) ribbon for board edge

1 Spread the royal icing on the cake board and sprinkle with brown sugar.

2 Roll the truffle paste into a sausage shape about 60cm (24in) long. Roll out 375g (12oz) of the pink sugarpaste into a long narrow strip and brush with water. Wrap around the truffle paste as shown, taking care to seal the join. Arrange the body shape in a coil on the prepared board. Shape the head from remaining pink paste and attach to the body. Shape the end of the tail to a point.

3 Cut out circles from yellow and green sugarpaste. Attach the yellow circles to the snake, and position a green circle on top of alternate yellow circles.

4 Shape eyes, nose and tongue from white, black and red paste, attach all parts to the snake. Trim the cake board with ribbon.

Place the rolled out truffle paste onto the prepared sugarpaste strip. Wrap the sugarpaste around, neatening the join as you go.

Very thinly roll out yellow and green sugarpaste and cut out two sizes of circles. The spots are attached to the body with a little water.

CUTE TEDDY

Always popular, this friendly teddy bear cake could be used for children's birthdays and christening celebrations.

1 large sphere-shaped sponge cake
1 medium sphere-shaped sponge cake
buttercream or jam for filling and masking
1.375kg (2¾lb) tan sugarpaste
reconstituted egg white
small amount of royal icing
30g (1oz) brown sugarpaste
7g (¼oz) black sugarpaste
22g (¾oz) black royal icing
peach dusting powder (blossom tint)

EQUIPMENT
30 × 25cm (12 × 10in) oval cake board
1 plastic cake pillar dowel (optional)
dusting brush
no. 2 piping tube (tip)
1 large ribbon bow

1 Split and sandwich the two sphere-shaped cakes with the chosen filling. The medium-sized cake may be left round, or you may prefer to sculpt the cake to more of an oval shape. Use a sharp knife dipped into warm water to make clean cuts. Chilling or part-freezing the cake prior to shaping makes the task easier. Mask each cake separately with buttercream or jam.

2 Roll out separate circles of tan sugarpaste and cover each prepared cake, smoothing the paste with the palms of your hands to create a neat finish. Attach the head to the body with reconstituted egg white or, to ensure that the cake is firmly attached, you may prefer to insert a plastic cake pillar dowel into the body and then push the head onto the dowel. Position on the cake board.

After shaping the cakes and spreading with buttercream, cover each shape with tan-coloured sugarpaste, then position the head on the body.

3 Shape two arms and two legs from the remaining paste and stick to the body with royal icing. Thinly roll out the brown-coloured paste and cut out two circles, attach to the legs as shown.

4 Thickly roll out some more tan paste and cut out a circle. Cut the circle in half and indent each with your thumb to form two ears. Stick them on to the head.

5 Using the dusting brush, apply a light blush of dusting powder to the cheeks as shown. It is a good idea to make a temporary 'bib' of absorbent kitchen paper for the teddy to catch any falling dusting powder that may otherwise stain the body.

6 Make two small flat circles of black sugarpaste for the eyes and a small oval for the nose, attach to the face. Pipe the mouth and stitching using a no. 2 tube (tip) with black royal icing. Attach the bow to the teddy's neck.

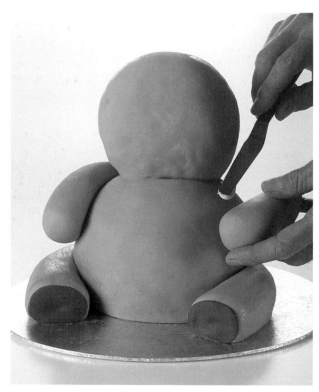

Shape the legs and arms from tan-coloured sugarpaste. While still pliable, attach to the body with dabs of tan-coloured royal icing or softened sugarpaste.

To prevent falling dusting powder settling on the sugarpaste surface, it is advisable to tuck a kitchen paper 'bib' under the teddy's neck.

RED AEROPLANE

A colourful novelty cake that will suit boys or aspiring pilots of all ages. Change the colours to suit the recipient.

500g (1lb) sponge loaf
buttercream or jam for filling and masking
315g (10oz) blue sugarpaste
125g (4oz) white sugarpaste
280g (9oz) red sugarpaste
15g (½oz) black sugarpaste
7g (¼oz) egg yellow sugarpaste
1 modelled marzipan or plastic pilot figure

EQUIPMENT
28cm (11in) cake board
oval cutter
small piece each red and black card
61cm (44in) ribbon for board edge

1 Roll out the blue sugarpaste and cover the cake board. Roll out the white paste to the same thickness as used to cover the board. Use the cloud template to cut out shapes from the blue paste in a random fashion over the board. Replace the removed blue with white cloud and smooth the joins with the fingers.

2 Using a sharp knife dipped in warm water, shape the sponge loaf as shown to form the body of the aeroplane. To make cutting easier and neater, chill or part-freeze the cake prior to shaping. Remove the cockpit using the oval cutter. Mask the cake shape with buttercream or jam.

3 Roll out 200g (6½oz) red paste and cover the body shape, trim the base and smooth the paste with the palms of the hands to create a neat finish. Place the cake across the board.

4 Make templates of the two wing shapes. Roll out the remaining red paste and cut out two of each wing shape. Attach to the aeroplane and board. Trace the tail shape onto red card and cut out neatly. Join to the aeroplane by gently inserting into the soft paste at the narrow end of the body

and the small rear wings. Roll out the black paste and cut out six small ovals for the windows. Position on the cake.

5 Make a tracing of the propeller on thin black card and cut out. Shape a flat circle of egg yellow paste. Attach both pieces to the aeroplane with dabs of icing. Sit the modelled marzipan or plastic pilot figure in the cockpit. Trim the cake board with ribbon.

After covering the board with blue paste, use the template to cut out cloud shapes which are then replaced with cut-out shapes of white sugarpaste.

Use a sharp bladed knife dipped into warm water to shape the body of the aeroplane. Remove a small oval of sponge for the cockpit using a cutter.

RED
AEROPLANE

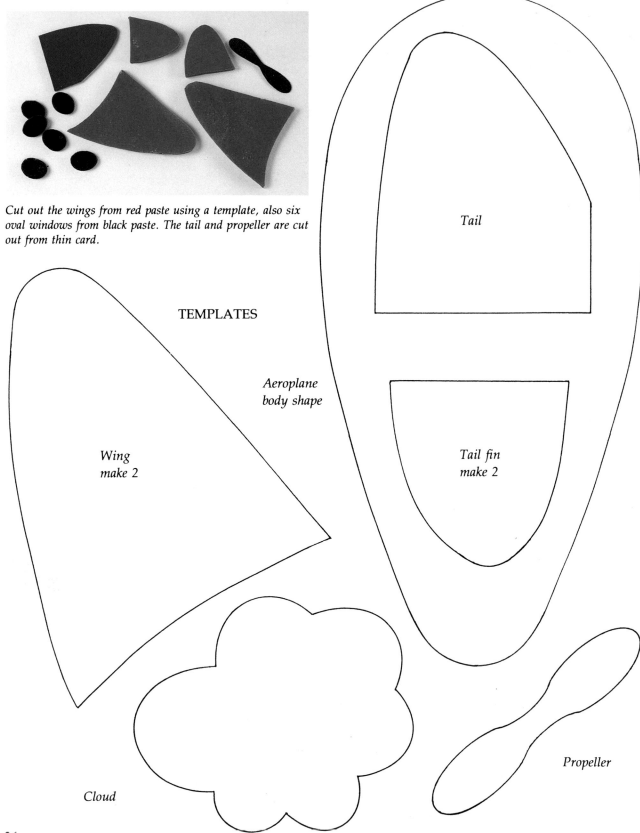

Cut out the wings from red paste using a template, also six oval windows from black paste. The tail and propeller are cut out from thin card.

TEMPLATES

Aeroplane body shape

Tail

Wing make 2

Tail fin make 2

Cloud

Propeller

YELLOW DINOSAUR

This multi-coloured species would certainly draw attention on a party table.

18cm (7in) round sponge cake
½ a small sponge layer or loaf cake
buttercream or jam for filling and masking
1.25kg (2½lb) lemon sugarpaste
60g (2oz) blue sugarpaste
280g (9oz) claret sugarpaste
22g (¾oz) each black and white sugarpaste

EQUIPMENT
45.5 × 20cm (18 × 8in) oblong cake board
130cm (52in) ribbon 7mm (¼in) wide for board edge

1 Split and sandwich the round sponge cake with chosen filling, then cut in half to form two semi-circles. Sandwich the two halves together, side by side, to form the basic body shape of the dinosaur. Shape the smaller cake into a cube for the head. Split and sandwich the cube of cake and arrange on the cake board with the body in a curved position. Mask the cake with buttercream or jam.

2 For the tail, take about 90g (3oz) of lemon sugarpaste and form a long carrot shape, attach to the body.

3 Reserve 125g (4oz) lemon paste, roll out the remaining paste and cover the cake. Place on the cake board. While still soft, indent the surface of the paste all over using the fingertips lightly pressed in.

4 Make balls of varying sizes from the blue sugarpaste, flatten and then press into the body and tail of the dinosaur.

5 Roll the claret paste into a long sausage and cut into pieces, graduating in size from small then large and back to small. Roll each piece into a ball, then shape into a squat carrot shape. Flatten the shape to form a spike. Repeat with each piece and attach to the body and tail in sequence of size.

6 For the legs, divide the remaining lemon paste into four pieces and shape as shown. Attach to the body.

7 Attach four flattened balls of yellow paste to the head, two for the eyes and two for the nostrils. Indent the nostrils with a fingertip. Roll the white paste into two ball shapes and attach to the eyes. Attach two smaller balls of black paste to the eyes. The mouth is made from a long thin strip of black paste attached to the head. Trim the cake board with ribbon.

Cover the prepared cake shapes with yellow sugarpaste and create the interesting texture by indenting the surface with the fingertips.

Cut out pieces of claret sugarpaste in graduating sizes, roll into squat carrot shapes and flatten. Attach along the back and tail with water.

JOLLY PIRATE

Any child will treasure memories of a party featuring this novel face cake, complete with spotted scarf and eye patch.

23 × 18cm (9 × 7in) oval sponge cake
buttercream or jam for filling and masking
410g (13oz) peachy-pink sugarpaste
140g (4½oz) purple sugarpaste
60g (2oz) each lemon and brown sugarpaste
45g (1½oz) each white and black sugarpaste

EQUIPMENT
28 × 23cm (11 × 9in) oval cake board
oval cutter

TIP

Don't worry if you don't have an oval tin to make this cake, it looks equally attractive made using a round sponge as the base – this also applies to the Rag Dolly cake on page 18.

---

1 Split and sandwich the sponge cake with chosen filling and mask with buttercream or jam.

2 Reserving a little for the nose, roll out the peachy-pink sugarpaste and cover the cake. Place on the cake board.

3 Thinly roll out the purple paste. Gently flatten balls of lemon paste onto the purple paste to form a regular pattern. Continue rolling the paste to create a smooth, spotted 'material' effect. Attach to the top of the face for a scarf. Cut the trimmings to form a tied knot.

4 Make the eye, nose, mouth and eye patch and attach to the cake. For the tufts of hair, model short pointed shapes of brown paste.

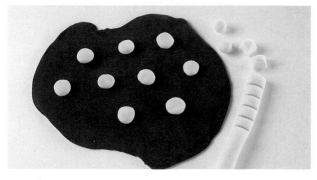

Thinly roll out the purple paste and polish the surface to remove excess icing (confectioner's) sugar before applying the yellow balls for spots.

Use cutters to make the eyes from white and black paste; the nose is modelled as a small oval ball. Use templates for the mouth and eye patch.

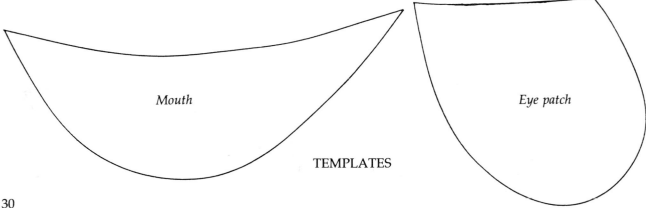

Mouth

Eye patch

TEMPLATES

GREY RABBIT

Both girls and boys would welcome the friendly smile of this cheerful rabbit at their birthday party.

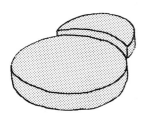

20 × 15cm (8 × 6in) oval sponge cake
13cm (5in) shallow round sponge cake
buttercream or jam for filling and masking
470g (15oz) grey sugarpaste
345g (11oz) white sugarpaste
100g (3½oz) pink sugarpaste
45g (1½oz) each brown, black, red and peachy-pink sugarpaste
60g (2oz) black royal icing

EQUIPMENT
45.5 × 30cm (18 × 12in) oblong cake board
no. 3 piping tube (tip)

1 Cut the oval sponge cake in half and sandwich with filling. Cut the small round cake into two semi-circles and sandwich with filling to make one deep semi-circle. Trim the cake to the same height as the oval cake and join together with buttercream or jam, as shown.

2 Use 220g (7oz) grey sugarpaste to cover the top part of the cake and cover the lower part with white sugarpaste, making a neat join where the two colours meet. Shape the grey paste at the join as shown in the main photo.

3 Roll out the remaining grey sugarpaste and use the template to cut out two ear shapes. Attach the ears to the head with water. Roll out the pink sugarpaste quite thinly and use a smaller template to cut out the inner ears. Attach to the grey ears with water. Bend over the tip of one grey ear.

4 Roll out the various colours of sugarpaste quite thinly and, using templates, cut out the various eyes, mouth, teeth and tongue shapes. Model a nose from the peachy-pink paste. Attach the pieces to the face with water. Using a no. 3 tube (tip) with black royal icing, pipe the outline of the mouth, the whiskers and eyebrows.

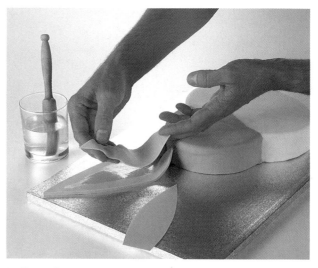

Roll out the grey paste quite thickly and use a template to cut out the ear shapes. The pink inlays use a smaller template and are attached with water.

Thinly roll out some white, black and pink sugarpaste and use templates to make the eyes and mouth. Shape a pointed ball of pink for the nose.

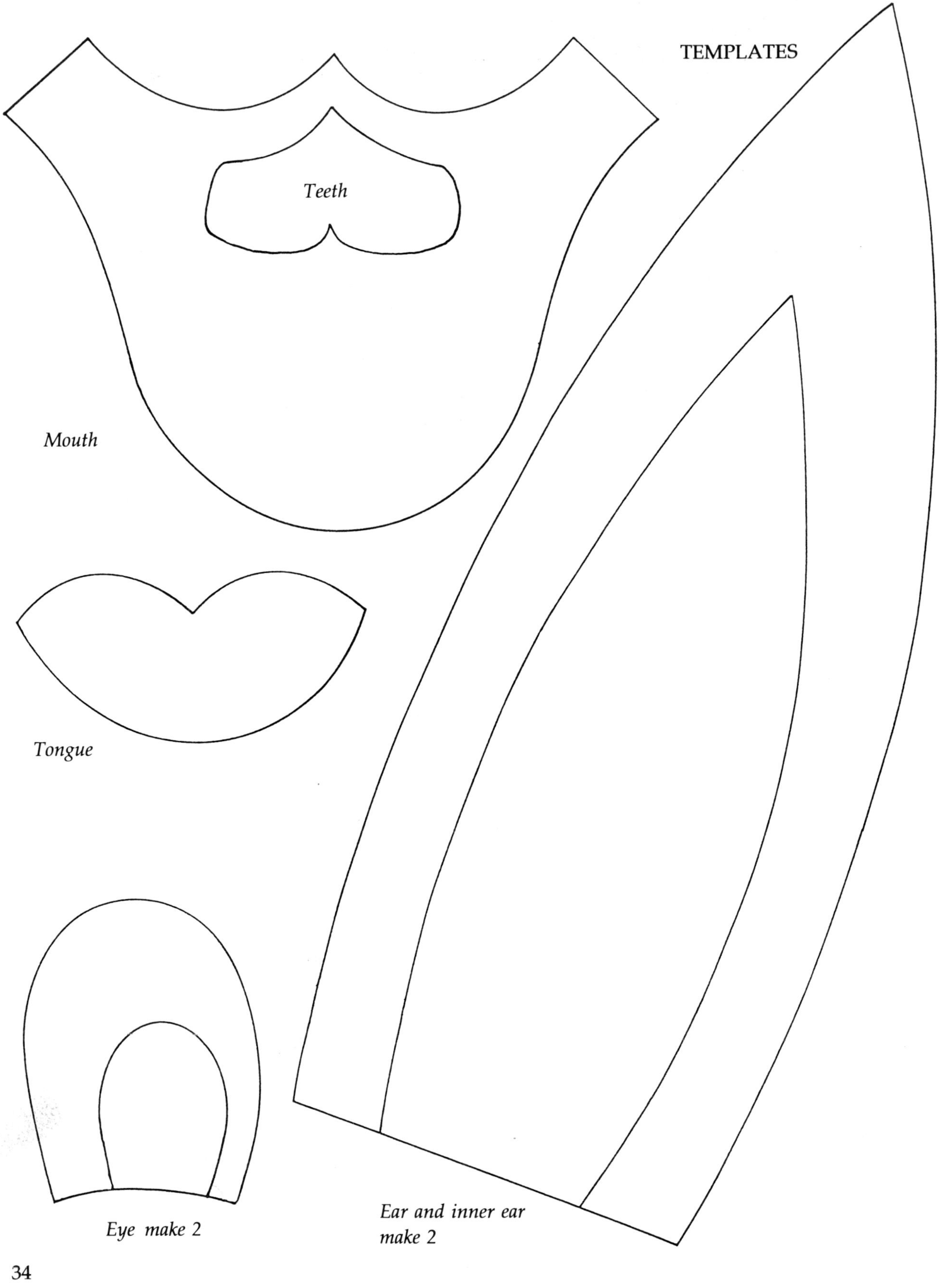

TEMPLATES

Teeth

Mouth

Tongue

Eye make 2

Ear and inner ear
make 2

34

BIRTHDAY EXPRESS

A dream come true for any young child hoping to be a train driver.

20cm (8in) square sponge cake
small jam-filled Swiss roll
buttercream or jam for filling and masking
470g (15oz) navy sugarpaste
185g (6oz) black sugarpaste
45g (1½oz) yellow sugarpaste
60g (2oz) each red, grey and white sugarpaste
60g (2oz) royal icing

EQUIPMENT
30 × 20cm (12 × 8in) oblong cake board
assorted round cutters
gold plastic bell
2 plastic 'Happy Birthday' writings
coloured sweets

1 Cut the sponge in half and sandwich with filling. Cut out as shown and assemble to form the basic shape, joining the parts together with buttercream or jam.

2 Cover the prepared engine shape with navy sugarpaste and position on cake board ready for decoration.

3 Cut the Swiss roll to the required length, about 9cm (3½in). If necessary, unroll the cake until the desired diameter of about 5.5cm (2¼in) is obtained. Cover the Swiss roll with navy sugarpaste and attach to the engine with royal icing.

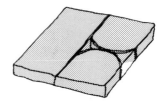

Use a sharp knife dipped into warm water to cut out the cake shapes. Sandwich with the chosen filling and assemble as shown.

Spread the small Swiss roll with buttercream or jam and position on a rolled out strip of blue sugarpaste. Roll up and neaten the join.

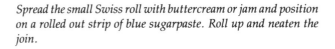

4 Roll out the black sugarpaste to a thickness of about 2.5mm (⅛in) and cut out a rectangle to form the roof, allowing about 5mm (¼in) overhang all the way around the roof. Attach to the cabin with royal icing.

5 Roll out the remaining black sugarpaste to a thickness of 1cm (⅜in) and cut out eight small wheels and two large wheels. Roll out the grey sugarpaste to a similar thickness and cut out two long bar shapes. Roll out the yellow sugarpaste and cut out the window shapes and the front plate. The boiler front is a circle of red sugarpaste, with the remaining red used to model the funnel.

6 Attach the various parts to the train with royal icing, waiting a few minutes to allow each part to set a little.

7 Attach the coloured sweets to the front of the train with royal icing and to each wheel, as shown. Attach the plastic bell behind the funnel and finish the cake with the plastic 'Happy Birthday' writings, attached to each side of the boiler with royal icing.

Roll out the various colours of sugarpaste and use cutters and templates to prepare the wheels, axles, window, roof and boiler front.

WHEELS TEMPLATE

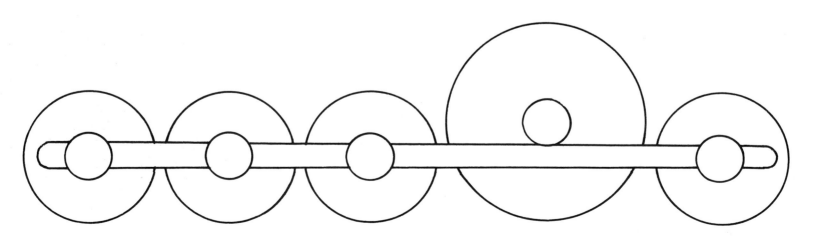

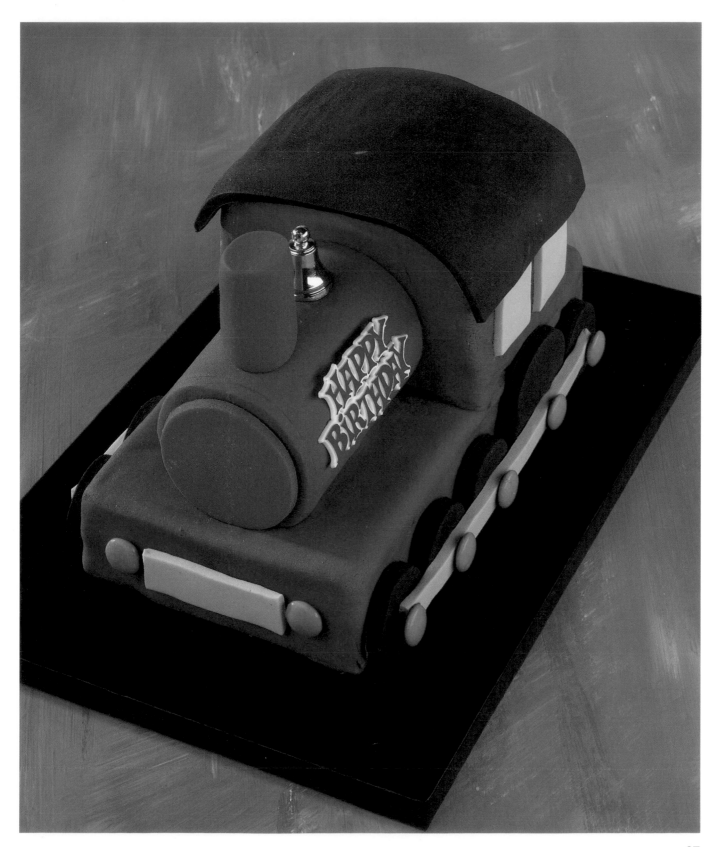

GREEN MONSTER

Not too frightening! This novelty cake would make an ideal centrepiece for a children's theme party.

15cm (6in) shallow round sponge cake
15cm (6in) square sponge cake
buttercream or jam for filling and masking
345g (11oz) green sugarpaste
60g (2oz) navy sugarpaste
30g (1oz) each white and black sugarpaste
30g (1oz) black royal icing

EQUIPMENT
30 × 25cm (12 × 10in) oblong cake board
paintbrush
oval cutter (optional)
round cutter (optional)
no. 2 piping tube (tip)

TIP

To avoid using two separate cake shapes, cut the monster's face out of an oblong sponge cake. The trimmings could be utilized as described on page 20.

1 Cut the round sponge in half and sandwich with filling. Split the square cake and sandwich with filling. Join the cakes as shown and mask with buttercream or jam. Cover the prepared shape with green sugarpaste and place on the cake board.

2 Using the template, cut out the hair from navy sugarpaste and attach to the head. Texture the hair with lines using the tip of a paintbrush handle.

3 Cut out the ears and shape the nose as shown from the green sugarpaste trimmings. Prepare the eyes, teeth and mouth from the white and black sugarpaste. Attach all parts to the cake with water. Pipe an outline around the eyes and corners of the mouth with the no. 2 tube (tip) and black royal icing.

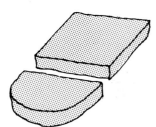

Use a card template to cut out the hair shape. The hair texture is created by making indented lines, using the rounded tip of a paintbrush handle.

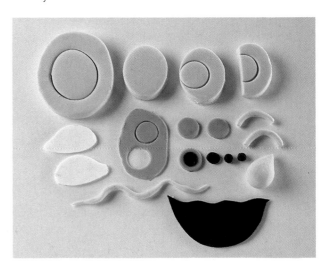

Make the eyes, nose, mouth and teeth by cutting the shapes from thinly rolled sugarpaste with the aid of templates; use a cutter for the ears.

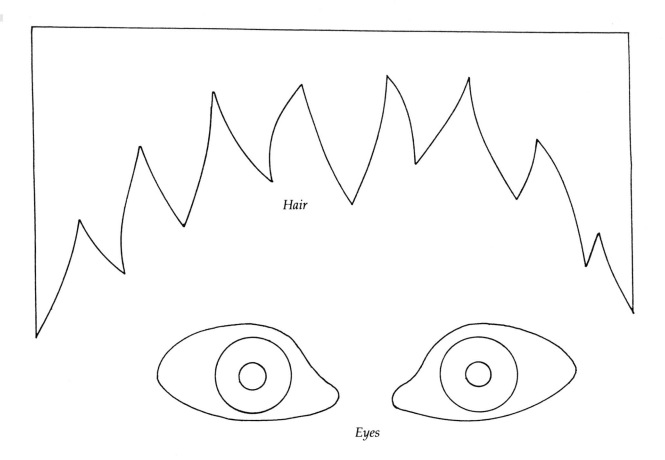

Hair

Eyes

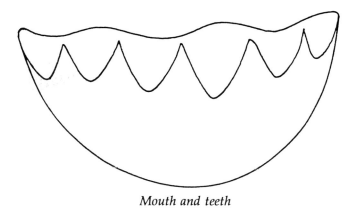

Mouth and teeth

MICE IN A BASKET

These two mice snug in a basket would make a lovely birthday cake for twins.

18cm (7in) round sponge cake
buttercream or jam for filling and masking
250g (8oz) chocolate sugarpaste
375g (12oz) coffee sugarpaste
185g (6oz) grey sugarpaste
15g (½oz) black sugarpaste
125g (4oz) pink sugarpaste
30g (1oz) royal icing

EQUIPMENT
25cm (10in) round cake board
basketweave rolling pin
string
ball modelling tool
no. 2 piping tube (tip)
about 90cm (1yd) ribbon for cake side and bow
about 90cm (1yd) ribbon for board edge

1 Cut the sponge cake in half and sandwich with filling. Spread the top and sides with masking material. Roll out chocolate sugarpaste and cover the cake. Place the covered cake on the cake board, positioning it slightly off-centre.

2 Roll out the coffee sugarpaste quite thickly and texture the surface with the basketweave rolling pin. Ensure that the paste is long enough to fit around the cake – measure the cake with string to give you an idea of the length required. Use a scalloped template to cut out the shape, moving the template along the paste to complete. Attach the piece to the cake side with water, neatening the join at the back of the cake.

3 Model the mice heads from the grey sugarpaste by making a large, pointed pear shape for each and, while the paste is still soft, indent the eyes using a ball modelling tool. Roll two ball shapes for the ears and press on a smaller ball of pink paste

Thickly roll out the light brown sugarpaste, texture with a basketweave rolling pin and scallop the edge using a template as a guide. Attach to the cake.

Model the heads from grey sugarpaste and pipe the eyes using white and black royal icing. Use a cocktail stick (toothpick) to make whisker marks.

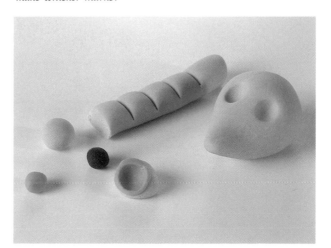

for the inner ear. Using the modelling tool, indent both together to create the finished ear. Attach the ears to the head with water. Using a no. 2 tube (tip) with white royal icing, pipe the eyes on, then roll two tiny balls of black sugarpaste and position on the eyes. Roll out two larger balls of black sugarpaste for the noses and attach in position with water.

4 Attach the ribbon and bow around the cake sides, ensuring that the bow is positioned at the front. Gather up any sugarpaste trimmings, knead together and model two pear shapes similar to those made for the heads but slightly smaller, attach the pieces to the cake top and press gently to flatten slightly – these will represent the bodies of the mice.

5 Roll out the pink sugarpaste quite thinly and cut out an 18cm (7in) circle, using a template, dinner plate or other suitable guide. Moisten the top area of the cake and the mice bodies and lay the circle on top, allowing it to find its own level. Fix the edges around the mouse heads to make them appear to be peeping from beneath. Attach ribbon to the board edge.

Thinly roll out some pink sugarpaste and use a template to cut out the large circle. Attach to the cake while still pliable.

FLOWER VASE

This colourful bunch of blooms in an edible vase would brighten a dull day, and is ideal as a Get Well or Thank You cake.

15cm (6in) long, 7.5cm (3in) diameter Swiss roll
buttercream for masking
345g (11oz) lemon sugarpaste
30g (1oz) chocolate sugarpaste
375g (12oz) white sugarpaste
paprika food colouring
gold dusting powder (petal dust/blossom tint)
confectioners' varnish (glaze)

EQUIPMENT
25 × 20cm (10 × 8in) oval board
chisel-head paintbrush
plastic posy spike
bunch of artificial tulips with leaves

TIP

If you are unable to obtain a suitable ready arranged bunch of flowers, purchase a selection of good quality fabric blooms and foliage and bind them together using florists' tape. Always use a posy spike when inserting wires into a cake.

1 Roll out the lemon sugarpaste and cover the cake board. Mix some paprika food colouring with water and paint a check design on the sugarpaste to represent a tablecloth.

2 Press out the chocolate sugarpaste into a circle and attach to one end of the Swiss roll with buttercream. Spread the sides of the Swiss roll with buttercream, then roll out the white sugarpaste and cover the Swiss roll making a protruding rim of paste at the covered end. Stand the roll upright. Gently press the plastic posy spike into the top of the vase.

3 Roll out the remaining sugarpaste into long narrow ropes and attach one to the base and one to the top of the vase with a little water. Attach the vase to the board with water.

4 Mix some gold dusting powder with confectioners' varnish (glaze) to a creamy consistency and paint the top and base rims of the vase and a decorative side design as shown.

5 Insert the bunch of flowers, securing with a small plug of sugarpaste.

Cover the cake board with yellow sugarpaste. Use a chisel-head paintbrush with paprika food colouring to paint on the tablecloth pattern.

Roll out three short sausage shapes of white sugarpaste and attach as shown to the top and base of the vase with a little royal icing.

Mix a little edible gold dusting powder with some confectioner's varnish and use a paintbrush to paint the pattern on the vase.

BOX OF CHOCS

This luxurious edible box of confections must be a chocaholics dream; alter the inscription to suit the occasion.

TEMPLATE

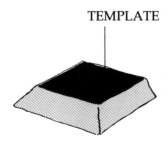

18cm (7in) square chocolate sponge cake
buttercream for filling and masking
440g (14oz) ivory pastillage
200g (6½oz) black sugarpaste
125g (4oz) red pastillage
185g (6oz) chocolate, melted
30g (1oz) black royal icing
assortment of luxury chocolates

EQUIPMENT
28cm (11in) square cake board
ribbed rolling pin
no. 1, 4 and 43 piping tubes (tip)
10cm (4in) gold thread
1.25m (1⅓yd) ribbon for board edge and bow

1 Roll out the black sugarpaste and cover the cake board. Cut the cake in half and sandwich with filling. Make a 15cm (6in) square template from thin card or paper and place centrally on top of the sponge cake. Use a sharp knife to champher the cake at an angle from the template edge to the outside base edge of the cake. Reserve the template for use later in step 2. Spread the top and sides with buttercream and place on the prepared cake board.

2 Make a template of the cake side shape and size. Roll out the ivory pastillage and texture the surface using the ribbed rolling pin. Cut out four side shapes, ensuring the ribbing runs in the same direction on all four sides. Attach to the cake and if possible, try to extend the sides about 5mm (¼in) above the height of the cake to create a box effect. Also cut out a square lid from the textured paste using the cake cutting template. Again, reserve the template.

3 Roll out the ivory pastillage trimmings thinly and cut out a rectangle for the gift tag. Cut a hole in the tag using a no. 4 tube (tip).

4 Add a few drops of cold water to the melted chocolate to thicken it slightly. Using a no. 43 tube (tip) with the prepared chocolate, pipe a shell border around the top and base edges and corners of the box. Pipe around the edge of the box lid.

5 Using a no. 1 tube with black royal icing, pipe an inscription of your choice onto the prepared gift tag. Knot the gold thread through the hole.

6 Roll out very thinly the red pastillage and cut out a square using the reserved template. Lay the square crossways on top of the cake to look like tissue paper lining. Arrange the chocolates in the box and attach the prepared gift tag and pink bow with melted chocolate. Trim the cake board edge with ribbon.

Roll out thickly the ivory-coloured sugarpaste and use a template to cut out the tapered edge strips which are then attached to the cake sides.

For the gift tag, roll out thinly some ivory sugarpaste and cut out a small oblong. Use a tube (tip) to make a hole for the tie and pipe on the inscription.

LET'S PARTY

Get in the party mood with this brightly coloured cake which, with a change of numerals, can be adapted for any age.

23 × 18cm (9 × 7in) oval sponge cake
buttercream or jam for filling and masking
750g (1½lb) lemon sugarpaste
90g (3oz) chocolate sugarpaste
30g (1oz) each white, red, yellow and blue pastillage
125g (4oz) yellow royal icing
30g (1oz) black royal icing
gold and silver edible food colouring

EQUIPMENT
33 × 28cm (13 × 11in) oval board
small oval cutter
small and medium star cutters
small alphabet cutters
large number cutters
no. 1 and 3 piping tubes (tips)
assorted colours of narrow gift or florists' ribbon
scissors
1m (1yd 3in) ribbon for board edge

1 Roll out thinly red, yellow and blue pastillage and cut out 15 oval shapes for balloons. Roll out white pastillage and cut out five small and five medium stars. Set aside on a flat surface to firm up.

For the balloons, roll out thinly some bright colours of pastillage paste and use a small oval cutter to make the shapes.

2 Roll out thinly the chocolate sugarpaste and use the small and large alphabet and number cutters to prepare the desired inscription, set the letters aside. Paint the prepared stars with gold and silver food colouring.

3 Cut the sponge cake and sandwich with filling. Mask the top and sides with buttercream or jam. Cover the cake with lemon sugarpaste. Cover the cake board with lemon sugarpaste and place the cake on top. Using tube (tip) no. 3 with yellow royal icing pipe a plain shell border around the base of the cake.

4 Attach the prepared lettering to the cake top with a little water or use tiny dabs of royal icing. Attach the balloons in groups of three around the cake side and the prepared stars with dabs of royal icing. Tilt the cake very carefully on a small box or other suitable object and using a no. 1 tube (tip) with black royal icing, pipe the balloon strings.

5 Cut the gift ribbon into short lengths and curl by pulling tightly against the blunt side of a scissor blade. Attach the ribbon curls with dabs of royal icing. Cover the board edge with ribbon.

Roll out some pastillage paste quite thinly and use a small star cutter to make the shapes. Paint the stars with edible gold and silver colour.

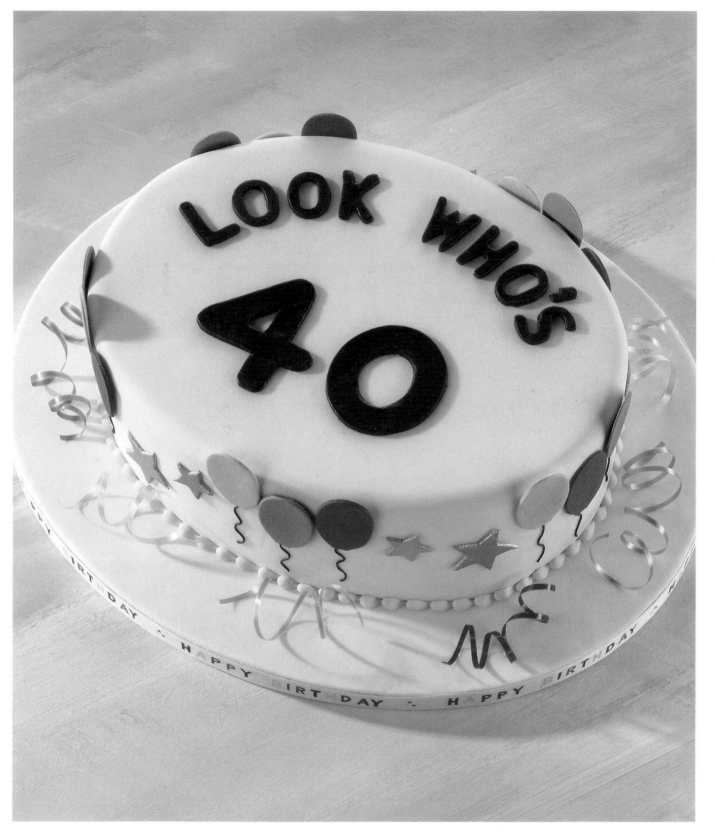

OWZAT CRICKET CAKE

Friends and family will be bowled over when they see this cricketer's cake for a sportsman's birthday.

TIP

The basic idea of this cake could easily be adapted to other sports by replacing the bails, wickets and ball with, say, a shuttlecock for badminton, crown green bowls or a squash racquet and ball. Change the wording for the recipient's name.

18cm (7in) square sponge cake
buttercream or jam for filling and masking
155g (5oz) blue sugarpaste
315g (10oz) cream sugarpaste
250g (8oz) green sugarpaste
90g (3oz) red sugarpaste
100g (3½oz) light tan sugarpaste
75g (2½oz) chocolate sugarpaste
30g (1oz) each white and black royal icing
confectioners' varnish (glaze), optional

EQUIPMENT
30 × 25cm (12 × 10in) oblong cake board
large alphabet cutters
no. 1 and 4 piping tubes (tips)
1.25m (1⅓yd) ribbon for board edge

1 Roll out the green sugarpaste and cover the cake board. Roll out the chocolate sugarpaste thinly and use the large alphabet cutters to make the 'OWZAT' inscription. Set the letters aside.

2 Cut the cake in half and sandwich with filling and mask the top and sides with buttercream or jam. Roll out the blue sugarpaste and cut out an 18cm (7in) square to cover the cake top and attach. Cut 30g (1oz) of the red sugarpaste into small pieces and roll each into a ball. Roll out the cream sugarpaste and press the red balls in a random pattern over the surface, re-roll to flatten the balls into the paste to make a spotted effect. Cut out four pieces to cover the cake sides and attach. Place the cake to one end of the cake board.

3 Roll the light tan sugarpaste into a long rope and cut to make three wickets, roll the rope a little narrower and cut two bails. Add thin ropes to each bail for detail and mark the wicket details with the back of a knife. If you wish, glaze the wickets with confectioners' varnish. Roll the

remaining red sugarpaste to make a half-ball shape. Use a no. 1 tube (tip) with royal icing to pipe the stitching on the ball.

4 Attach the wickets, bails and ball to the cake top with water. Use a no. 4 tube with black royal icing to pipe the movement marks near the wickets and ball. Position the lettering and trim the cake board edge with ribbon.

Roll out some dark brown sugarpaste and use large biscuit (cookie) cutters to make the 'Owzat' inscription. Attach to the sugarpaste-covered cake board with water.

Make the wickets, bails and half-ball from coloured sugarpaste. Glaze all pieces with confectioner's varnish to add a sheen.

TROPHY CAKE

This cake will be a real winner for any achievement celebration and can be easily adapted to suit the occasion.

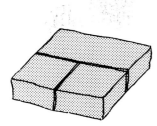

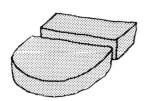

18cm (7in) round sponge cake
18cm (7in) shallow square sponge cake
buttercream or jam for filling and masking
545g (1lb 1½oz) grey sugarpaste
185g (6oz) black sugarpaste
60g (2oz) red sugarpaste
30g (1oz) royal icing

EQUIPMENT

38 × 36cm (15 × 14in) oblong cake board
Garrett frill cutter or round fluted cutter and small round cutter
cocktail stick (toothpick)
no. 2 piping tube (tip)

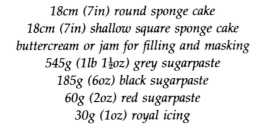

1 Cut the round cake in half and sandwich with filling to make a semi-circle. Cut the square cake as shown and attach the piece to the semi-circle with buttercream or jam. Join the remaining pieces with buttercream or jam and cut to form the plinth shape. Mask both cakes with buttercream or jam. Roll out 220g (7oz) grey sugarpaste and cover the cup. Roll out the black sugarpaste and cover the plinth. Position the two cakes on the cake board.

2 Divide the remaining grey sugarpaste into three. Roll two pieces into long tapering ropes and curve them to make two handles. Model the stem shape from the third piece of paste, attach all pieces to the cup and plinth with water. Roll out the black sugarpaste trimmings, cut out a narrow strip for the plinth detail and attach with water.

3 Roll out the red sugarpaste and cut out two pieces to represent ribbon tails for the rosette. Also, cut out a fluted circle and a smaller circle. Place a cocktail stick (toothpick) on the edge of the circle, press gently and roll the stick from side-to-side to frill the edge of the paste. Attach the tails

to the cup with water, followed by the fluted circle and finally the small circle. Using a no. 2 tube (tip) with white royal icing, pipe on the '1st' lettering.

After shaping the cakes and spreading with a buttercream or jam masking, cover the cup with grey sugarpaste and the base with black paste.

Roll out short, slightly tapered sausage shapes of grey sugarpaste, then curve and shape to form the handles. Attach to the cake with a little water.

Thinly roll out some red sugarpaste and cut out a fluted circle to make the rosette. Frill the edges using a cocktail stick (toothpick) and add two tails.

DIY CAKE

Any practically-minded person would admire the detail on this novelty. Use the idea for a birthday or Father's Day cake.

30 × 25cm (12 × 10in) shallow oblong sponge cake
buttercream or jam for filling and masking
315g (10oz) coffee sugarpaste
125g (4oz) light brown sugarpaste
250g (8oz) chocolate sugarpaste
155g (5oz) grey sugarpaste
125g (4oz) black sugarpaste
45g (1½oz) black royal icing

EQUIPMENT
33 × 20cm (17 × 8in) oblong cake board
ribbed rolling pin
zigzag cutter
no. 2 piping tube (tip)
30cm (12in) light tan florists' ribbon
scissors

1 Cut the cake in half lengthways to make two long rectangles, sandwich together with a filling and mask the top and sides with buttercream or jam.

2 Layer the coffee sugarpaste and light brown sugarpaste on top of each other and press together. Cut into slices and rearrange together, gently pressing into one mass. Roll out the paste to create a streaky, wood grain effect, then texture the surface with a ribbed rolling pin. Use the prepared paste to cover the top and four sides separately. Place the cake on the cake board.

3 Roll out the grey sugarpaste and using a template or a zigzag cutter, cut out the saw blade and set square blade. Model the saw handle, using the template as a guide, and the hammer shaft from chocolate sugarpaste. Model the hammer head from the remaining grey paste and the set square handle from black paste. Attach all parts to the cake with water.

4 Use the black sugarpaste trimmings to make small balls, then flatten the balls and, with a no. 2 tube (tip) with black royal icing, pipe spikes on to make nails. Attach the nails to the cake with water. Cut the florist ribbon into four long lengths and then into various shorter pieces, curl by pulling tightly against the blunt side of a scissor blade. Place the curls around the cake board to represent wood shavings.

Roll out grey sugarpaste and use a template or zigzag cutter to make the saw blade. Model the saw, hammer handles and hammer head from coloured paste.

Make several small balls of black sugarpaste and flatten slightly. Using a no. 2 tube (tip) with black icing, pipe short spikes to make 'tacks'.

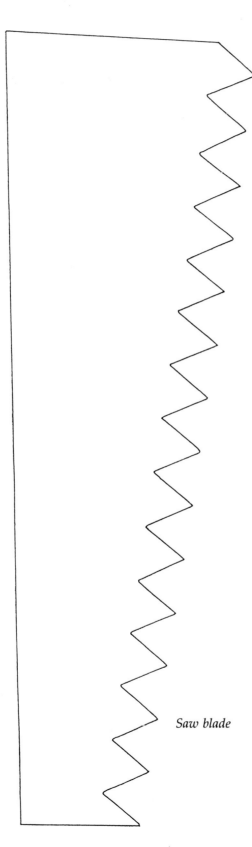

Saw blade

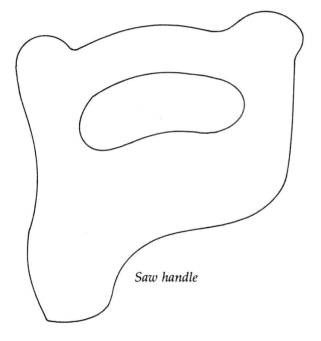

Saw handle

FUCHSIA CAKE

The graceful elegance of these hanging blooms lend themselves ideally to the triangular shape of this cake.

25 × 20cm (10 × 8in) shallow sponge cake
buttercream or jam for filling and masking
685g (1lb 6oz) pale pink sugarpaste
125g (4oz) royal icing
lavender food colouring
pink, violet and green edible painting colours

EQUIPMENT
triangular cake board
large carnation cutter or 3.5cm (1½in) fluted round cutter
no. 1 piping tube (tip)
1m (1yd 3in) ribbon for cake side
fuchsia design stencil
1m (1yd 3in) ribbon for board edge
paintbrush

Roll out pink sugarpaste and use a large carnation or small fluted round cutter to make the border pieces, cut in half and attach at the base of the cake.

> **TIP**
>
> To ensure a neat and professional finish is achieved, it is worth taking the time to arrange the cut-out border shapes alongside the cake and check the spacing between each piece is equal before sticking them to the board.

1 Roll out 280g (9oz) of the pale pink sugarpaste and cover the cake board, trimming the edges neatly. Cut the cake as shown and join together with buttercream or jam to make a triangular shape. Mask the top and sides with buttercream or jam. Roll out 345g (11oz) pink sugarpaste and cover the cake. Place cake on prepared board.

2 Roll out the remaining pink sugarpaste and use the carnation cutter to cut out several fluted circles. Cut each circle neatly in half with a small sharp knife. Make three circles with a vee shape cut out to fit the angle of the pointed corners. Attach the pieces to the cake board with water. Using a no. 1 tube with lavender-coloured royal icing, pipe a small, plain shell border around the base of the cake where the fluted semi-circles join the cake side. Attach a narrow ribbon and bow to the cake side, securing the join at the back with a dab of royal icing.

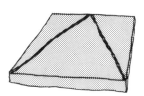

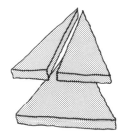

After stencilling, the icing should dry quickly. Paint the flowers with violet and the foliage with green food colouring using a fine paintbrush.

3 Place the stencil on the cake top and, using a small palette knife, spread royal icing across all the cut outs and carefully remove the stencil. Trim the board edge with ribbon.

4 Make a tracing of the inscription and pin-prick onto the cake top. Pipe the inscription using the same lavender icing and tube as before. Using a fine brush with edible paint food colourings, paint in the coloured detail on the raised icing of the stencilled motif.

The lettering shown on the cake is piped on using a no. 1.5 tube (tip) with slightly softened royal icing. As an alternative, choose from a range of bought plastic lettering.

TEMPLATES

Flower stencil design

Lettering

PEACH DRAGEE CAKE

The gold dragees just add a special sparkle to this delicately coloured cake suitable for any occasion.

20cm (8in) hexagonal rich fruit cake covered with marzipan (almond paste)
60g (2oz/¼ cup) boiled apricot jam
125g (4oz) marzipan (almond paste)
clear alcohol (gin or vodka)
625g (1¼lb) peach sugarpaste
about 100 gold dragees
60g (2oz) peach royal icing

EQUIPMENT
25cm (10in) hexagonal cake board
plastic ruler
nos. 1 and 2 piping tubes (tips)
tweezers (optional)
about 90cm (1yd) ribbon for board edge
about 90cm (1yd) lace for board edge
wired spray of peach flowers and ribbon loops

1 Use the ruler to indent lines from point to point on the cake top by pressing gently. Take a sharp knife and neatly cut any one of the six sections and remove the wedge to leave a space. The removed wedge can be sliced and wrapped to make extra portions. Brush the exposed cut surfaces of the fruit cake with apricot jam and cover with the rolled out marzipan, neatening the joins and edges.

2 Brush the marzipan with alcohol and cover the cake with peach sugarpaste. Whilst the sugarpaste is still soft, mark the quiltwork pattern with the ruler on the top and sides of the cake as shown in the photo.

3 Using a no. 1 tube (tip) pipe tiny dots of royal icing where the quiltwork lines cross and attach a gold dragee on each – if you find the dragees difficult to pick up and position, use tweezers. Position the dragees before the icing sets.

4 Roll out the remaining peach sugarpaste to cover the cake board, position the cake and trim the board edge with ribbon and lace. Pipe a small, plain shell border around the base of the cake using a no. 2 tube (tip) with peach royal icing. Attach the spray of flowers in the cut away area with a spot of royal icing.

Immediately after covering the cake, and while the paste is still soft, mark the diagonal quilt pattern using a ruler or royal icing smoother.

Using a no. 1 tube (tip) with peach royal icing, pipe a tiny dab of icing into each cross of the quilting. Attach the dragees using tweezers.

GOLD DRAPE CAKE

An unusual colour scheme that creates a really rich and sophisticated look to this cake for any occasion.

25cm (10in) shallow round rich fruit cake covered with marzipan (almond paste)
clear alcohol (gin or vodka)
410g (13oz) cream sugarpaste
625g (1¼lb) navy sugarpaste
185g (6oz) pastillage
gold dusting powder (petal dusts/blossom tints)
confectioners' varnish (glaze)
30g (1oz) royal icing

EQUIPMENT
33cm (13in) round cake board
1m (1yd 3in) ribbon for board edge
paintbrush
6 navy ribbon bows
small plastic vase (see step 4)
wired arrangement of cream flowers and navy ribbon loops

TIP
To achieve a good golden colour and to make painting easier, mix the edible gold dusting powder with confectioner's varnish (glaze) to a creamy consistency and use immediately.

1 Brush the marzipan with alcohol and cover the top of the cake with a large circle of cream sugarpaste. Make the circle large enough to curve over onto the top of the cake side. Roll out 280g (9oz) of navy sugarpaste into a long narrow strip to cover the cake's side. Attach to the cake and neaten the join where the two colours meet.

2 Cover the cake board with the remaining navy sugarpaste and position the cake. Trim the board edge with ribbon, then mark the cake's circumference into six equal divisions.

3 Roll out a sixth of the pastillage very thinly and cut into a 13.5 × 9.5cm (5¼ × 3¾in) rectangle. Working quickly, brush both short sides with a little water and fold the piece to form neat pleats. Pinch the two ends firmly and attach to the cake with water, arranging the drape to form a nice curved shape. Repeat around the cake with the five remaining portions of pastillage.

4 If the atmosphere is dry, the pastillage will set quickly. If in doubt, dry under the warmth of a desk lamp. Mix gold dusting powder with confectioners' varnish to a creamy consistency and paint the drapes. If you wish, paint the vase.

5 Attach the ribbon bows to the drapes with royal icing. Fix the flowers securely into the vase and position on the cake top.

Very thinly roll out some white pastillage paste and use a template to cut out an oblong shape. Cut out and work one section at a time.

Without delay, before the paste starts to crust, moisten each short end with water and fold the piece concertina fashion into neat pleats.

Again, working quickly with the piece before it starts to crust, pinch the two short ends gently to secure the pleats, then attach to the cake.

GARLANDS AND BOWS

The increasingly popular petal shape of this cake lends itself beautifully to the draped garland decoration.

20cm (8in) petal-shaped rich fruit cake covered with marzipan (almond paste)
clear alcohol (gin or vodka)
875g (1¾lb) ivory sugarpaste
90g (3oz) lavender sugarpaste
90g (3oz) ivory royal icing

EQUIPMENT
30cm (12in) petal cake board
about 1.5m (1⅔yd) ribbon for board edge
clay gun/sugar shaper with clover leaf-shaped blade
no. 2 piping tube (tip)
wired posy of lavender fabric flowers and ribbon loops
plastic posy spike

1 Brush the cake with clear alcohol and cover with ivory sugarpaste. Trim away any excess paste. Cover the cake board with sugarpaste and place the cake on it. Trim the board edge with ribbon.

2 Using the ivory sugarpaste trimmings, fill the clay gun and then fit the clover leaf-shaped blade. Squeeze out a short length of paste, and whilst still soft, twist neatly and attach to the cake with water to form a curved garland effect. Repeat around the cake. Using a no. 2 tube (tip) with ivory royal icing, pipe a plain shell border around the base of the cake.

3 Roll out the lavender sugarpaste thinly and use templates to cut out the bow and tails shapes. Moisten the centre of the bow with a little water and fold the two ends in. Cover the joint with a small rectangle of sugarpaste. Attach two tails to the back of the bow and then attach the bow to the cake with water at the join of the garlands. Repeat around the cake.

4 Press the plastic posy spike into the cake and insert the flower arrangement, securing with a little royal icing.

Thinly roll out some lavender coloured sugarpaste and use a small card template to cut out the bow pieces. Fold as shown and attach to cake.

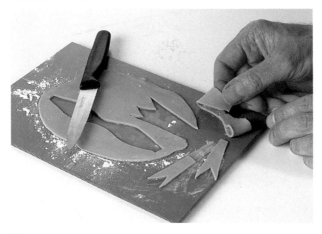

Use a sugar shaper gun with ivory sugarpaste to extrude short lengths of ribbed paste. Neatly twist before attaching to the cake.

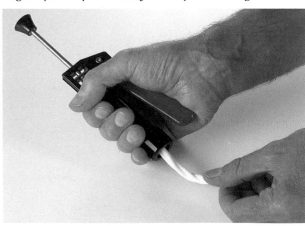

BLACK AND WHITE CAKE

Something different . . . this cake could be used as a centrepiece for a party table for any adult celebration.

20cm (8in) square rich fruit cake covered with marzipan (almond paste)
clear alcohol (gin or vodka)
575g (1lb 2½oz) white sugarpaste
105g (3½oz) black sugarpaste
30g (1oz) grey royal icing
150 silver dragees
pink foil-covered chocolate spheres

EQUIPMENT
28cm (11in) square cake board
no. 1 piping tube (tip)
30cm (12in) ribbon for champagne glass
champagne glass

1 Reserve 60g (2oz) each of white and black sugarpaste. Divide the white into two pieces and shape into a rough oblong, shape the black into an oblong and sandwich between the two pieces of white. Roll up Swiss-roll fashion and cut into slices. Group the pieces together in a random fashion and roll out to give a streaky, marbled effect. Brush the cake with alcohol and cover with the prepared paste. Trim away any excess paste from the edges and place the cake centrally on the cake board.

2 Take the reserved white and black sugarpaste and roll each out into two long narrow ropes, twist together and roll slightly to neaten. Attach the twisted rope to the base of the cake with water, trim and join neatly at the back of the cake.

3 Using a no. 1 tube (tip) with grey royal icing, pipe random groups of three small dots and single dots over the top and sides of the cake, attaching a silver dragee to each dot. Pipe a few at a time otherwise the icing may dry before you have attached the dragee.

4 Tie the ribbon in a bow around the stem of the champagne glass. Position the glass in the centre of the cake and pile with pink foil-wrapped chocolate spheres.

Take similar amounts of white and black sugarpaste and roll out slightly. Layer together, then roll up Swiss roll fashion ready to use.

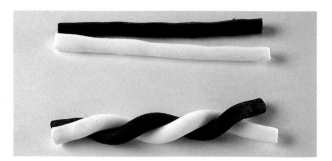

Roll a long narrow sausage of white and black sugarpaste and twist together to form a neatly striped border. Attach to the cake with water.

FILIGREE FANTASY

An unusual idea for a celebration cake that would certainly create a talking point for a girl's 21st party.

medium 15cm (6in) diameter sphere-shaped rich fruit cake covered with marzipan (almond paste)
875g (1¾lb) pink sugarpaste
clear alcohol (gin or vodka)
90g (3oz) royal icing

EQUIPMENT
28cm (11in) round cake board
1m (1yd 3in) silver banding
no. 1 piping tube (tip)
selection of pink and white fabric flowers, beads, wired gypsophila and ribbon loops
florists' tape
silver plastic 21 numeral
2 tulle butterflies

1 Use 250g (8oz) of pink sugarpaste to cover the cake board, Brush the cake with alcohol, roll out the remaining pink sugarpaste and cover the cake. Position the cake off-centre on the cake board and attach with royal icing.

2 Using a no. 1 tube (tipe) with royal icing, pipe filigree work all over the cake. Filigree is simply an irregular pattern of small m's and w's all joined together without the starts and ends of the piping being noticeable. Also, pipe a scalloped line around part of the cake board edge (see main photograph).

3 Prepare a selection of flowers as shown and wire them into a crescent arrangement tapering in size at each end. Secure together with florists' tape. Attach the spray of flowers to the cake board with a dab of royal icing.

4 Press the plastic numeral into the soft sugarpaste covering on the cake board and attach the butterflies to the cake with dabs of icing. When moving the cake, take great care as the weight may cause it to topple over.

After covering the sphere cake with pink sugarpaste, position off-centre on the prepared cake board ready to commence the decoration.

Using no. 1 tube (tip) with white royal icing, pipe fine filigree all over the sphere-shaped cake.

Prepare the ribbon loops, gypsophila and fabric flowers ready for wiring and taping into a crescent arrangement for the cake board.

PINK ROSE HEART

This simple cake could be used for various occasions such as birthdays, engagements or anniversaries.

20cm (8in) heart-shaped rich fruit cake covered with marzipan (almond paste)
1kg (2lb) pale pink sugarpaste
60g (2oz) white sugarpaste
clear alcohol (gin or vodka)
pink and claret food colouring
7 pink wafer roses
pink dusting powder (petal dust/blossom tint)
15g (½oz) royal icing

EQUIPMENT
28cm (11in) heart-shaped cake board
1m (1yd 3in) ribbon for board edge
small piece of cloth
small and large crimpers
paintbrush
5 green fabric leaves
plastic 'With Love' writing

TIP

If you think the ragging technique may be too time-consuming for you, cover the cake and cake board with marbled sugarpaste as described on page 66 but replace the black and grey sugarpaste with two shades of pink.

---

1 Brush cake with alcohol and cover with pale pink sugarpaste. Use the remaining pink sugarpaste to cover the cake board.

2 On a plate mix a small amount of pink food colouring with some clear alcohol, scrunch up a small piece of cloth and dip into the mixed colour, dab the cloth gently onto the sugarpasted board in a random pattern to create a 'ragging' effect. Repeat the technique with claret colour. Colour the sugarpasted cake in the same way.

3 Place the cake on the cake board and cover the board edge with ribbon. Roll out the remaining pink sugarpaste into a long narrow rope, attach to the base of the cake with water. Use the large crimping tool to make a decorative pattern on the rope.

4 Roll out the white sugarpaste and use a template to cut out a heart shape slightly smaller than the cake. Use the small crimper to create a

decorative edge around the heart shape and attach to the cake top with a little water.

5 Brush the edges of the wafer rose petals with pink dusting powder, remove the outer petals from two flowers to create buds. Arrange the flowers and leaves on the cake top with the plastic writing and attach with royal icing.

Mix a little pink food colouring with a small amount of alcohol. Using a small piece of screwed-up fabric, lightly dab the sugarpaste in a random fashion.

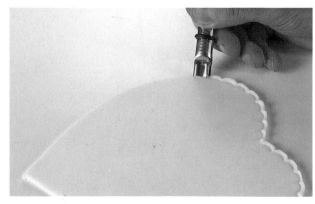

Immediately after cutting out the shape and before the paste begins to crust, use a crimping tool to create a decorative edging around the heart.

CONFETTI CAKE

A really unusual, modern shaped cake decorated with traditional bridal confetti that's also edible!

1 large dome-shaped, rich fruit cake covered with
marzipan (almond paste)
60g (2oz/¼cup) boiled apricot jam
185g (6oz) marzipan (almond paste)
clear alcohol (gin or vodka)
750g (1½lb) pale green sugarpaste
selection of dusting powders (petal dusts/blossom tints)
in lemon, pink, mauve, peach, green and blue
icing sugar
3 A4 size sheets wafer (rice) paper
90g (3oz) royal icing

EQUIPMENT
25cm (10in) round cake board
two 15cm (6in) round cake boards
about 90cm (1yd) pale green ribbon for board edge
2m (2yd 6in) each lemon, pink, mauve, peach, blue and
white satin ribbon, 3mm (³⁄₁₆in) wide
flower wires
florists' tape
plastic posy spike
tweezers
three 8.5cm (3½in) round white plaster cake pillars

1 Cut the fruit cake about one third of the way down to make a small top tier with a base diameter of 15cm (6in) and a larger bottom tier. Brush the cut edge of larger cake with apricot jam and cover with marzipan (almond paste). Brush the cakes with alcohol. Place the smaller cake on a cake board and cover with pale green sugarpaste, covering the board edge completely. Trim the edges. Place the bottom tier on the large cake board and cover the cake and exposed rim of the cake board with pale green sugarpaste, trimming the edge neatly. Trim the board edge with ribbon.

The cake is baked in a special shaped tin as shown and cut to form a small top tier and a base tier. Cover the cakes with marzipan and sugarpaste.

TIP

During preparation of the edible confetti, take care to avoid the rice (wafer) paper coming into contact with moisture or steam, which will soften and distort it. For the same reason, it is advisable to pick up the confetti and attach to the cake using tweezers in case of moisture on the fingertips.

2 Mix a small amount of coloured dusting powder with a little icing sugar to the desired tint, rub the mixture gently into the rough side of half a sheet of rice (wafer) paper. Repeat on the remaining half sheets of paper with the other colours. Make templates of the confetti shapes, trace onto the rice paper and cut out a selection of colours and shapes.

3 Cut the ribbon into 1m (1yd 3in) lengths. Make a loop at one end and secure with a short length of flower wire. Tape the join with florists' tape and repeat with the remaining ribbon. Group all wires together and secure with tape to make a loopy bow with trailing tails.

4 Gently press the plastic posy spike into the centre of the small cake. Place the second small cake board on the top of the large cake and secure with royal icing, then position the three cake pillars. Place the top tier on the pillars and fix the prepared ribbons into the posy spike securing with royal icing, with the lengths flowing down the cake sides.

5 Fix the prepared confetti to the cake and bottom board with dabs of royal icing, mixing the colours and shapes as you work.

Prepare the rice (wafer) paper as described and use the templates and small scissors to cut out the heart, bow, bell and horseshoe shapes neatly.

TEMPLATES

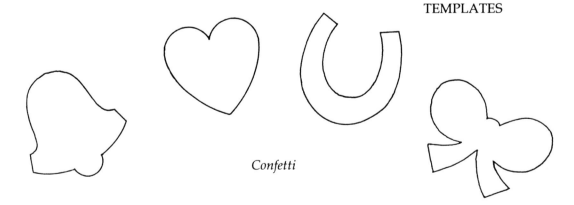

Confetti

RUBY ANNIVERSARY

This cake is made more interesting by the simple cut away corner section which features a keepsake of the occasion.

20cm (8in) square rich fruit cake
1kg (2lb) marzipan (almond paste)
boiled apricot jam
clear alcohol (gin or vodka)
1.25kg (2¼lb) ivory sugarpaste
100g (3½oz) ivory royal icing
9 small edible red roses with leaves

EQUIPMENT
28cm (11in) square cake board
crimper
oval cutter
no. 2 and 3 piping tubes (tips)
gold plastic 'Congratulations' writing
plastic 4 and 0 numerals
1.25m (1⅓yd) red velvet ribbon for board edge

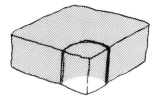

1 Make a card template from the drawing provided and use as a guide to cut a curved section from a corner of the fruit cake. Brush the cake with apricot jam and cover with marzipan (almond paste) in the conventional manner. Brush the marzipan with clear alcohol and cover with ivory sugarpaste. Cover the board with ivory sugarpaste and place the cake on top.

2 Using the ivory sugarpaste trimmings roll out a long narrow rope and fix to the base of the cake with water. Make a decorative pattern on the rope using a crimper. Using a no. 2 tube and ivory royal icing, pipe a decorative line around the edge of the board.

3 Roll out thickly the remaining small piece of sugarpaste and cut out an oval shape, position in the cut out area on the cake board and attach with water. Insert the plastic numerals into the oval base.

Thickly roll out some ivory pastillage and use an oval cutter to make the base for the plastic numerals.

TIP

The basic design of this cake can easily be adapted for other anniversaries – simply change the colour of the flowers and cake board edging and replace the numeral and inscription if necessary with a silver one.

4 Make a template for the linework design and place on the cake top. Using a no. 3 tube (tip) with ivory royal icing, pipe a line around the cake top. Using a no. 2 tube with the same icing, pipe a line on each side of the no. 3 line and a line on top of the no. 3 line.

5 Attach the roses to the cake top and bottom corners with royal icing, also attach the plastic writing with tiny dabs of icing. Trim the cake board edge with ribbon.

Make a template from thin card or paper and place on the cake top. Using no. 3 and no. 2 tubes (tips) with ivory royal icing, pipe tiered linework.

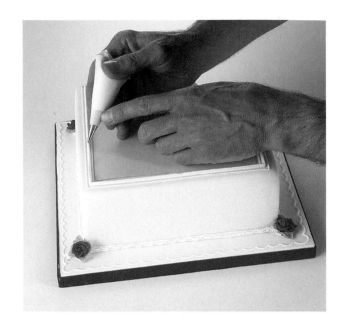

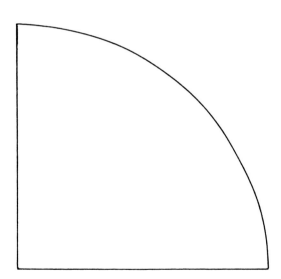

Corner cut out

STORK CAKE

A quick, neat decoration for an attractive Christening cake that can easily be adapted for a girl by changing the colours.

20cm (8in) square rich fruit cake
75g (2½oz/¼cup) boiled apricot jam
1kg (2lb) marzipan (almond paste)
clear alcohol (gin or vodka)
560g (1lb 2oz) aqua sugarpaste
30g (1oz) white sugarpaste
60g (2oz) royal icing
blue and paprika edible painting colours

EQUIPMENT
28cm (11in) square cake board with the corners removed
stork design stencil (see also page 96)
small palette knife
1m (1yd 3in) blue ribbon for cake edge
12 white fabric blossoms
8 blue fabric filler flowers
8 ribbon loops
natural dried gypsophila
tweezers
fine brush
4 blue ribbon bows

TIP
To ensure a perfectly flat cake top surface is achieved, which is essential to good stencilling, gently press a cake board or rolling board onto the sugarpaste immediately after covering and smoothing are completed and before the sugarpaste starts to skin over.

1 Measure in 3cm (1¼in) from each corner of the fruit cake and make a mark with a knife. Using the marks as a guide, cut a triangle off each corner of the cake. Brush the cake with apricot jam and cover with marzipan (almond paste) in the conventional manner. Brush the cake with alcohol and cover with aqua sugarpaste. Trim the edges and place on the cake board.

2 Place the stencil on the cake top and using a small palette knife, spread royal icing across the cut out of the stencil. Carefully remove the stencil.

3 Using a fine brush and the edible paint food colourings, paint in the coloured detail on the raised icing of the stencilled motif. If you prefer to avoid painting, apply different colours of royal icing at the stencilling stage.

4 Cover the bottom of the cake with blue ribbon, joining the ribbon at one corner. Make four small balls of white sugarpaste and attach one to each corner of the cake board. Divide the flower selection into four and insert a group of flowers and ribbons into the paste at each corner using tweezers. Attach a ribbon bow to each cake side with a dab of royal icing.

Place the stencil flat on the cake top, positioning it with an even margin all around. Use a small bladed cranked palette knife to apply the icing.

Make small balls of white sugarpaste and attach to cake board with a dab of royal icing. Using tweezers for ease, insert the flowers and ribbon.

ANNIVERSARY BELL

Shaped cake tins are now widely available – try a bell shape to make a stunning cake for a Golden Anniversary.

1 medium-size bell-shaped rich fruit cake covered with marzipan (almond paste)
clear alcohol
440g (14oz) egg yellow sugarpaste
30g (1oz) ivory sugarpaste
30g (1oz) royal icing

EQUIPMENT
20cm (8in) round gold cake board
23cm (9in) round gold cake board
25cm (10in) round gold cake board
2.5m (3yd) gold banding
double-sided adhesive tape
crimper
oval cutter
no. 1 piping tube (tip)
18cm (7in) strung gold beads
gold plastic 50 numeral
plastic posy spike
wired crescent spray of yellow fabric flowers, gold leaves and ribbon loops

Cover the cake with marzipan and sugarpaste and position on the prepared stepped cake boards. While the paste is soft, use a crimper to make a fancy edging.

1 Trim the edges of each cake board with gold banding and attach them together in a tiered fashion using double-sided tape. Brush the cake with alcohol and cover with egg yellow sugarpaste, trim away the excess paste and place the cake on the prepared stepped cake boards. Make a decorative edge as shown around the lower part of the bell using a crimper while the paste is still soft.

2 Roll out the ivory sugarpaste and cut out an oval shape. Using a no. 1 tube (tip) with royal icing, pipe a line around the edge of the oval shape and attach the gold beads, pressing gently into place. Attach the plastic numeral with tiny dabs of icing and attach the finished plaque to the cake with royal icing.

3 Push the plastic posy spike into the top of the cake and insert the wired flower arrangement and the ribbon loops, securing with a plug of sugarpaste.

Thinly roll out some ivory pastillage and cut out an oval shape. Using no. 2 tube, pipe a line on the edge and attach the gold beads as shown.

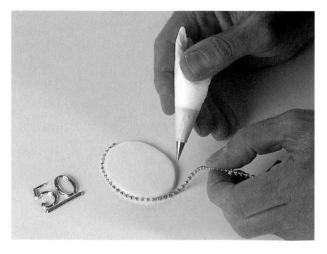

BRODERIE CAKE

A simple yet beautiful cake that could be used as a pre-wedding celebration cake or for engagement celebrations.

20cm (8in) shallow round rich fruit cake covered with marzipan (almond paste)
clear alcohol (gin or vodka)
410g (13oz) white sugarpaste
90g (3oz) royal icing
peach food colouring

EQUIPMENT
30cm (12in) round cake board
broderie cutter
no. 0 and 1 piping tubes (tips)
about 1.5m (1⅔yd) strung plastic pearls
about 51cm (24in) peach ribbon, 7mm (¼in) wide
selection of white and peach fabric flowers, beads, gypsophila and ribbon loops
2 silver plastic wedding rings

1 Make a template of the scalloped pattern so it is ready to use. Place the marzipanned cake centrally on the cake board and brush with clear alcohol. Also slightly moisten the cake board nearest to the cake. Roll out the white sugarpaste large enough to fit over the cake and onto the board. Cover the cake in the conventional manner and smooth the paste onto the cake board – do not trim at this stage. Place the template over the cake and on the sugarpasted board. Using a small knife, carefully cut the scalloped edge pattern, lift off the template then remove any excess sugarpaste.

2 Cut out the broderie pattern from each scallop section, if the pieces stick in the holes use a cocktail stick (toothpick) to remove them.

After covering the cake and board with sugarpaste, and while still soft, use a template to cut out the fancy scalloped design on the cake board.

Again, while the paste is still soft, use a special broderie anglaise cutter to remove the cut-out design in each section of the scallop.

3 Using a no. 1 tube (tip) with white royal icing, pipe a line on the edge of the scalloped sugarpaste, attach the pearls, pressing gently into place. Colour a little royal icing peach and use a no. 0 tube (tip) to pipe the outline of each broderie hole.

4 Attach the ribbon to the base of the cake with a dab of icing. Roll out the remaining sugarpaste and cut out a 15cm (6in) circle using a template or saucer, attach to the cake top, slightly off-centre, with royal icing and finish the edge with pearls as in step 3. Attach a small ball of sugarpaste to the circle and insert the flowers, beads, gypsophila and ribbon loops to make a pleasing arrangement. Attach the two intertwined wedding rings with dabs of icing.

Using a no. 2 tube (tip) with white royal icing, pipe a line on the scalloped paste edge. Attach the beads by gently pressing into the icing.

TEMPLATE

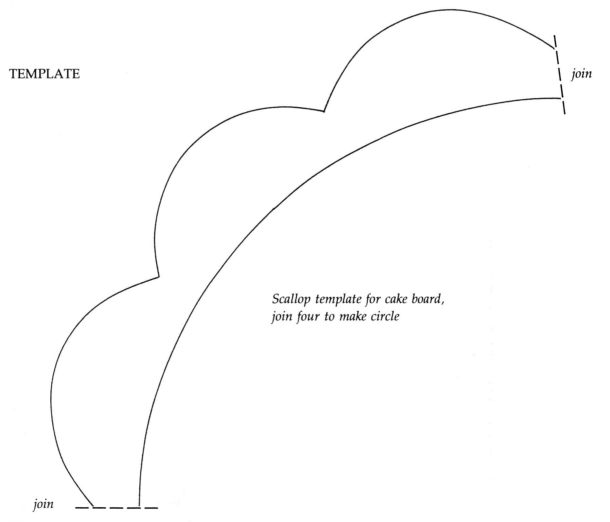

join

join

Scallop template for cake board, join four to make circle

join

HAPPY SANTA

An alternative to the traditional rich fruit cake, this novelty would also make a nice edible gift.

25 × 20cm (10 × 8in) shallow sponge cake
buttercream or jam for filling and masking
345g (11oz) red sugarpaste
45g (1½oz) peach sugarpaste
125g (4oz) black sugarpaste
155g (5oz) white sugarpaste

EQUIPMENT
triangular cake board
ribbed rolling pin
1 small holly and berry piquet

1 Cut the cake as shown and join together with buttercream or jam to make a triangular shape. Mask the top and sides with a thin layer of buttercream. Roll out the red sugarpaste and cover the cake, trim off the excess.

2 Roll out the peach sugarpaste and cut out an 8.5cm (3½in) diameter circle using a card template or suitably-sized kitchen container. Cut out the same shape from the red sugarpaste covering on the cake and replace with the prepared peach circle, smooth the join where the two colours meet. Place on the cake board.

3 Reserve a pinch of black sugarpaste for the eyes and shape the remainder into two oblong blocks, attach to the base of the cake and bend to represent two boots.

4 Roll out 125g (4oz) white sugarpaste and use the template to cut out the beard shape. Texture with a ribbed rolling pin and attach the beard to the body with water.

5 Prepare the off-pieces by rolling out the sugarpaste and cutting out the white and black eyes. Model a nose from peach and a moustache, hat brim and bobble from white as shown. Model a mouth from red sugarpaste. Attach all parts to the cake with water. Attach holly piquet to the hat.

Cut out and remove a circle of red paste as shown. Roll out and cut out a circle of flesh colour paste to fit in the gap. Smooth the join with the fingertip.

Roll out some white sugarpaste and, using the template, cut out the beard shape. Carefully lift onto the cake and attach with a little water.

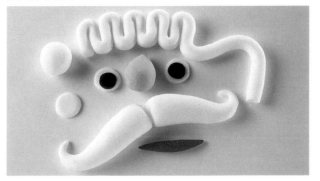

Prepare the eyes, nose, hat trim, bobble and curly moustache from sugarpaste. Attach the pieces to the cake with water.

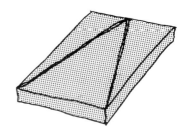

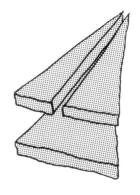

Beard

FESTIVE CANDLE WREATH

Friends and family will gasp with amazement as you bring this lighted to the dinner party table.

TIP

Should you have more time available and wish to add more detail to this cake, you can further enhance the decoration shown by introducing red, green or gold ribbon loops and artificial pine cones and Christmas roses in between the holly and berries.

18cm (7in) chocolate sponge ring
buttercream for filling and masking
185g (6oz) chocolate sugarpaste
75g (2½oz) green pastillage
45g (1½oz) red sugarpaste
orange and brown dusting powders (petal dusts/blossom tints)
16 gold foil-wrapped chocolate spheres
small amount of melted chocolate

EQUIPMENT
23cm (9in) round gold cake board
large holly leaf cutter
piece of aluminium foil
paintbrush
twisted gold candle
three white fabric flowers
red ribbon for the board edge

1 Cut the ring cake in half and sandwich with buttercream. Mask the surface of the cake with a thin layer of buttercream.

2 Roll out the chocolate sugarpaste and cover the cake. Trim any excess paste from the base edge and place the cake on the cake board. Trim the board edge with red ribbon.

3 Roll out the green pastillage and cut out holly leaves using the cutter, set the leaves in crumpled foil and leave to firm up. Divide the red sugarpaste into small pieces and roll into balls for berries.

4 Tint the holly leaves by brushing with orange and brown dusting powder. Take the chocolate sugarpaste trimmings and knead together, fix into

the centre of the ring with royal icing and press the candle in position. Attach the leaves, berries and foil-wrapped chocolates to the cake with melted chocolate. Add the white fabric flowers to the centre of the wreath.

Bake the cake in a ring mould. It can be fruit cake with marzipan or a simple sponge spread with a masking. Cover the cake with brown sugarpaste.

Roll out some green pastillage quite thinly and use a large size holly cutter to make leaf shapes. Place the shapes on crumpled foil to firm up.

POINSETTIA TREE

The rich traditional colours of this stylish tree cake will add a real festive touch to your Christmas table.

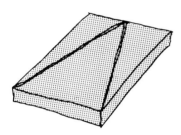

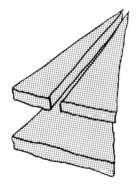

TIP

If time is limited or to avoid buying the necessary cutter just for a 'one-off' cake, you could replace the edible hand-made poinsettia with a good quality fabric bloom from your local florist or craft shop.

25 × 20cm (10 × 8in) shallow sponge cake
buttercream or jam for filling and masking
375g (12oz) moss green sugarpaste
75g (2½oz) red pastillage
7g (¼oz) yellowy-green sugarpaste
30g (1oz) royal icing
10 gold dragees

EQUIPMENT
triangular cake board
ribbed rolling pin
large holly leaf cutter
paintbrush
2 medium holly and berry piquets
1 small holly and berry piquet
5 artificial spruce sprigs
1 gold card star
1 tartan ribbon bow

1 Cut the cake as shown and join together with buttercream or jam to make a triangular shape. Mask the top and sides with buttercream. Roll out the green sugarpaste and cover the cake. Texture the top only with the ribbed rolling pin, then trim off the excess paste. Place on the cake board.

2 Roll out the red pastillage and cut out several holly leaf shapes. If you wish, mark the veins using the back of a knife.

3 Roll out a short rope of green sugarpaste and attach to the top of the cake with water to form a ring and attach a small ball of paste in the centre. Arrange the red petals in two layers attaching with water. Roll small balls of yellowy-green sugarpaste, indent slightly with the handle of a paintbrush and attach to the flower centre.

4 Arrange the holly piquets, spruce sprigs, dragees, gold star and tartan bow attractively on the cake and attach with dabs of royal icing.

Prepare the cake as described, cover with green sugarpaste in the conventional manner, then texture the surface with a ribbed rolling pin.

Roll out the red pastillage and polish the surface with the palms of your hands to remove excess icing (confectioner's) sugar. Use a large holly leaf cutter to make the poinsettia petals.

Roll a short sausage shape of green sugarpaste and attach to the cake with water. Press a small ball of paste in the centre and attach the petals.

HAPPY NEW YEAR

Rich colours and a traditional thistle decoration make a spectacular cake to cut when the clock strikes midnight.

TIP

If you don't fancy piping the clock numerals and inscription, use readily available edible or plastic lettering and numerals available from good sugarcraft shops.

25 × 20cm (10 × 8in) oval rich fruit cake covered with marzipan (almond paste)
clear alcohol (gin or vodka)
750g (1½lb) claret sugarpaste
250g (8oz) deep green sugarpaste
60g (2oz) white sugarpaste
60g (2oz) royal icing
30g (1oz) black royal icing
wired spray of fabric eryngium thistles, small and large berries and ribbon loops

EQUIPMENT
33cm (13in) round cake board
1m (1yd 3in) ribbon for board edge
68cm (27in) tartan ribbon
scriber or hat pin
no. 1 piping tube (tip)
small piece of gold card

1 Roll out deep green sugarpaste and cover cake board. Brush cake with clear alcohol and roll out claret sugarpaste. Cover the cake in the conventional manner and place slightly off-centre on the prepared cake board. Trim the cake board edge with ribbon and position tartan ribbon around the base of the cake, join and secure at the back of the cake with a dab of royal icing.

2 Roll out the white sugarpaste thinly and, using a template, cut out the oval clock face shape. Attach to the right-hand side of the cake top with water. Make a tracing of the inscription and position on cake top, pin-prick each letter onto sugarpaste covering. Using a no. 1 tube (tip) with royal icing slightly softened with a few drops of cold water, pipe on the inscription.

Cover the cake with marzipan and claret sugarpaste in the conventional manner. Position the cake on the dark green sugarpasted cake board.

Position the tartan ribbon around the cake, join and secure at the back of the cake with a dab of royal icing.

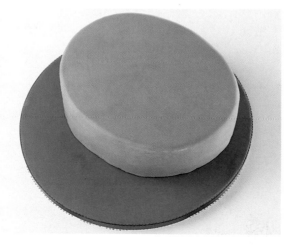

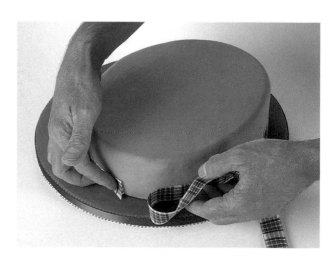

3 Using a no. 1 tube with black royal icing, pipe the numerals on the clock face and edge the oval shape with a scalloped line. Cut out the clock hands from gold card and attach to the clock with a dab of icing. Position the wired flower and foliage spray and attach to the cake board with royal icing.

Make a tracing of the lettering and use a hat pin or scriber to pin-prick the design onto the cake. Pipe on the inscription.

TEMPLATES

Clock face

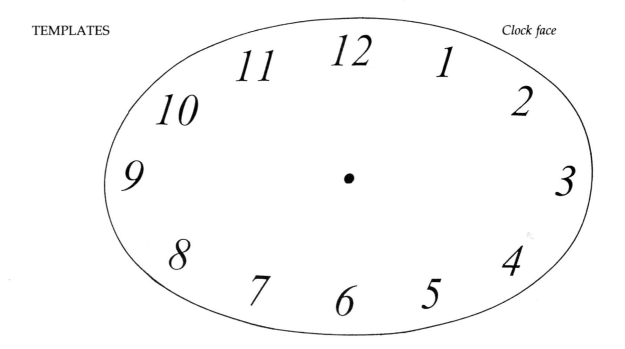

Lettering

Facial features

Hair (left)
reverse template for
right hand side

Trace the design shown onto thin card or acetate. Cut out using a sharp craft knife.